THE GOD BOX

My Life as Elvis

JEFFREY "ELVIS" FULLNER

MIRACLE ENTERTAINMENT PROMOTIONS

THE GOD BOX

My Life as Elvis

This is an MEP Publication

Miracle Entertainment Promotions

For information contact :
P.O. Box 62, Lynden, WA 98264
www.jeffreyelvis.com

Book and Cover design by Jeffrey Elvis Fullner
Book Formatting layout by Derek Murphy @Creativindie
Photography Lynde Dorscher
ISBN-13 : 978-1984929969
ISBN-10 : 1984929968
First Edition: January 2018

DEDICATED TO MILITARY VETERANS
OF BOTH THE U.S. AND CANADA

And to all my wonderful fans who have supported me across North

America through thick and thin

We have such a brief time upon this earth, and yet, there is time enough for everything that is important. Too much time is spent worrying about the things that make no difference at all.

—JEFFREY "ELVIS" FULLNER

CONTENTS

FORWARD

The Resemblance

O N A BUSY DIESEL SATURATED TAR FLAT, somewhere in the Midwest on a turnpike overpass truck stop, I stood patiently in the blistering heat, pouring several hundred gallons of fuel into the polished silver tanks bolted to the side of my big rig semi-truck.

"Hey mister, did anyone ever tell you that you look just like

Elvis Presley?" said a middle-aged man, a short distance away in the next pumping lane of the Flying 'J' truck stop. His curved brim red and white cap shadowed his reddened sun-bleached face. It had been stamped with a screen-printed trucking emblem, probably from the outfit he was driving for. It was an all too familiar greeting I was still struggling to get used to, especially at six a.m. in the morning, before I even had time to comb my hair or sip my morning cup of coffee.

"Yeah, I hear that a lot," I replied with a smile. "Thank you very much," he said attempting a crude imitation of the King. The trucker smiled and pointed his index finger in my direction as I headed back to the cab.

As I walked away, trying not to show my embarrassment, his driving partner rolled down the window and yelled, "Elvis has left the building," and gave me a 'thumbs up' as I drove away from the long covered fueling terminal.

Do I look like Elvis? I don't know—but I've heard that a lot over the last few years since I grew my sideburns out while I was driving truck in 2007 at the peak of the Great Recession. My intent wasn't really to look like Elvis Presley at all, but the attention did add an interesting touch to my daily hauling routine; at least it made for some very interesting conversation.

When I began writing down the stories based on my experiences as a rookie coast-to-coast truck driver and my transformation toward becoming a professional entertainer; I wasn't exactly sure where I was going to go with this story. When I start a journey, I don't always sit down and draft a careful map of where I'm going, so the path of discovery is often as exciting for me as it is for those around me. The same could be said for the road trips during my years as a truck driver, although I wouldn't normally admit that I didn't always know where I was going, especially to my dispatcher at the central Salt Lake terminal.

However, somewhere around the middle of writing the stories for this book, it occurred to me the coincidences of my adventures as a truck driver had crossed paths with Elvis in many ways; especially the drive that had taken me to the west coast of Florida looking for a sandy beach to get some sun. I imagined myself driving over the same bridge that was featured in an Elvis motion picture produced near Yankeetown Florida in 1961. Yankeetown was a quaint little town along the coast in the middle of nowhere, yet it was here in front of that small karaoke audience that I discovered that I really did look and sound just like Elvis Presley and that I just might have what it takes for becoming an Elvis Tribute Artist.

The events in this story took place over the course of a two-year period I spent driving a long-haul truck across forty states; 100,000 miles of interstate highway and country roads. The characters are as authentically portrayed as I can remember.

The influences the amazing pastor Jeremiah serving the 'All Nations Assembly of God Church' in Albuquerque New Mexico had a profound influence on my life at the time. In that brief encounter, when my truck was delayed during a routine layover, I took a driving break in a dusty scorched red desert parking lot where I spent some time with this extraordinary preacher and his congregation. It wasn't the words in his sermon that got my attention—the sermon wasn't that great, to be honest. It was the confidence in his words and his determination to speak the Word of God, "until the day he dies," that spoke to me. When he does finally die, I have no doubt this Navajo Indian pastor will continue his message well into the afterlife, just as he said.

His stories of persecution are something most of us can't relate to and it was obvious to me that his conviction and his personal life as a new Navajo Christian, had shaped his ministry forever as the pastor in this small, multi-culture missions church. When I left the church, I shook the pastor's hand and said, "Yes sir, I will follow my dream."

Okay, I know—you want to know about Elvis. Of course— most people aren't that interested in Jeffrey as I discovered in the many years I've tried to make it as an original songwriter, musician. My intrigue with Elvis began with a simple birthday card my wife and kids gave me for my forty-second birthday on my first solo long-haul trip across the country. Hours of staring at the Elvis photo on the flimsy glossy card hanging from my dashboard, gave birth to an obsession of intrigue that impacted my decision to start singing again. I felt I had to know what it was like to be a neon superstar.

What drove Elvis? What motivated him? What was he really

like outside of the media hype? Might I have what it takes to be like him? I have only scratched the surface to what Elvis experienced and achieved in his incredible twenty-year career. My walk down the path in his shoes was only a blip in comparison, but it continues to be an incredible journey of discovery.

THE GOD BOX

CHAPTER ONE

Learning the Ropes

I T WAS TO BE MY FIRST, late night cross-country drive, working for a large conglomerate Salt Lake refrigerated trucking company. I had decided somewhere along the thousands of miles of tar and dusty interstate roadways of North America to start memorizing Elvis songs, hoping to one day, become a professional singer; that's if I was ever able to get off this truck. It's funny the things you think about when you are three-thousand miles from home driving down the highway ten to twelve hours a day. I spent considerable time thinking about what I would do if I ever got another chance to live a normal life. As my thoughts drifted far away to my home in the small Dutch town of Lynden, Washington where I lived with my family. My life had been sadly trimmed financially, reduced overnight to an empty shell by what was to become known as the Great Recession.

But, tonight I was listening to an Elvis favorite on the XM satellite radio. I turned up the volume focusing on careful control over my vocal chords as I began to sing "Only Fools Rush In". Together Elvis and I filled the cabin with legendary and timeless music; while my CDL driver-trainer lay sound asleep in the sleeper bunk loft just behind my seat.

The highway traffic was not heavy at 2 a.m. driving across the state of Indiana headed north for an early morning load up close to the town of Appleton, just west of Lake Michigan. Like most of the towns we drove through, I had never heard of Appleton, so every town I visited was an adventure in seeing new places and territory I had never seen before. As I ground my shifter all the way into tenth gear, I heard my trainer grumble from his bunk as the grinding steal gears made contact creating an awful sound resembling a bad toothache being drilled at the dentist. I had yet to perfect the art of gliding the gears in smoothly, but I knew after several hundred thousand miles behind the wheel I would eventually get the hang of it; just wouldn't be today, not by a long shot.

Driving an eighteen-wheeler was somewhat of an adventure to me since there was so much of the country I had never seen. The scenery along the way was incredibly beautiful. I was only beginning to appreciate the vastness of the North American continent as my travels covered seemingly endless distances every day. My appreciation for the beauty of our nation grew each day from sunrise to sunset, or sunset to sunrise, sometimes both; twenty-four hours a day.

Long-haul truck driving does as it turns out, have a dark side; as I discovered the hard way. Driving nights is a tough job and it is extremely hazardous, especially in the wee hours of the morning. At least once a week I would look out the window and see fragments of a semi-truck, often not recognizable from a distance. Intuitively, you knew that not everyone walked away from the accident and I couldn't escape the thought that my number might be coming up soon. At night in the broken remains of a tragic accident, you could see the black glossy stains of what you could only imagine was there before emergency crews arrived to clean up the debris and remains; hauling them all away in black sealed hazardous containment bags.

Tonight, like most nights, my stomach felt empty. I tried to hold off eating snacks as long as I could. I don't remember ever being overweight in my whole life, but I was gaining weight rapidly since I had very little to do during the long hours the truck rolled down the road twenty-four hours a day, seven days a week. When you drive with a partner, the truck never stops except for unloading and refueling at truck stops. The truck is in motion all the time and even rest breaks are kept short to keep ahead of the demanding delivery schedules.

I thought it was odd that an amateur driver like myself would be trained under such stringent circumstances, but I never complained because I knew that when this was all over, I would be able to handle driving any schedule the company could throw at me; which later proved to be true. The aggressive training would give me a healthy driving advantage over drivers that were not pushed to their limits during the seven-week training period. I was grateful.

I reached over and picked through the stations on my satellite radio finding a talk show. I decided on a religious station thinking the stimulation of conversation would keep me awake for a few more hours as the dim glow of another hot summer day began to emerge from the eastern horizon over Lake Michigan. The incredible lake seemed to stretch forever in all directions as we followed the coast, almost like an ocean. The moon touched the shimmery waves as it glided quietly into the horizon and not even the lights at night could be seen on the other side, hidden by the curvature of the earth.

I am pretty sure my diet conscious wife would not have approved of my diet, but the fruits and vegetables she had packed for me after my last visit home was long gone and I was left to gather whatever I could find to eat at the truck stops. My coffee had now been cold for several hours, but I thought it would be best if I finished the large plastic mug of what can only be described as black oil which would be the perfect topping for the jalapeno chip dip, the fried chicken, and several small bags of sunflower seeds I had devoured earlier.

The glow of the sunrise over the eastern horizon was an amazing spectacle as it began to brighten the day. It saddened me to think that such a simple pleasure could only be seen in the wee hours of the morning; a wonderful pleasure experienced by few as the early morning sky, full of stars to the west were slowly gobbled up by the gleaming rays of red and gold tentacles that seemed to reach across the sky like a living creature climbing out of the trenches of darkness, to start another day. It was hard not to stare out of the passenger window at the incredible display of light and shadows; beginning a day I probably wouldn't remember, in a place I would soon forget.

A teardrop began to form in the corner of my eye from the long-night stress of not sleeping. I reached up and whisked it away only to discover a tiny formation of sand around my eyelids just beginning to develop. I was exhausted, but it would only be a few hours before my shift would be over. I was hoping to make it through to Milwaukee before changing drivers, so I would have time for a nice breakfast before heading back to the rear bunk to start my scheduled rest. There's nothing like a big plate of bacon alongside an egg and trucker sized biscuits with gravy; a meal that could put any man into a coma for hours while the vibration of the deep tread all weather tires and the powerful pulse of the diesel refrigerator engine behind your bunk, lulls you sound asleep, much like a baby in a wooden carriage on a red brick road.

By the feel of the rugged road under my wheels, I knew we had crossed the border into Illinois. My confidence for driving was growing and I felt I would eventually make a good driver. It was a good decision to take this job and I really loved this truck.

I managed to grind out another gear reaching close to the truck's internally regulated speed at sixty-two miles per hour; we were making good time. As I rounded a long slow corner, I could see a small commotion just a short distance in front of me. Traffic congestion had picked up suddenly. I was out in the middle of nowhere, rolling along with a full heavy load in the right lane while faster trucks passed me on the left side. I unexpectedly caught up with a truck ahead of me that looked like he was slowing down for some reason. Concerned, I began fumbling through the gears to start decelerating the heavy load; I needed time to stop if there was an emergency ahead. A reason to stop didn't seem likely because it was pitch black dark and there were still no city lights in view.

Now there were less than two truck lengths ahead of me and it appeared something was seriously wrong. Suddenly the driver in the truck ahead of me jetted over to the adjacent lane to the left of me and slammed on his brakes. Blue smoke billowed from the rear tires that were almost completely locked from the emergency braking system. His trailer made a loud bang as the air braking mechanism released tons of pressure into the cylinders that abruptly slowed the empty box truck with thousands of pounds of heart-stopping force.

The commotion set off sparks on the roadway that had momentarily distracted my attention from the impending disaster closing in on me, just ahead. It was then that I realized why the truck had changed lanes. My lane had come to a complete stop and I was now headed for an imminent impact with another box truck blocking my lane. There simply was no place to go and at my current speed, I would probably be sitting in the front seat of the truck ahead of me before the one I was driving stopped. I thought of the black hazardous waste bags and the faces of the emergency crews cleaning up messes no one should ever have to see. With a sudden jerk reaction, I slammed on my air breaks with everything I had in me while gripping the heavy truck wheel and giving it a good hard crank to the right. I didn't know what was out there on the right side of the road but thought this would be a good time to take the risk since this lane change would likely be my last.

The maneuver worked, but in the darkness, I could see nothing. My mirror barely grazed the trailer of the truck on the left, bending it ever so slightly as I steered off the road narrowly avoiding a collision. I watched helplessly as a mile marker sign disappeared under the heavy weight of the front tire. In the chaos, I caught the glimpse of a startled deer, its glowing eyes reflecting the glow of my high beam headlights. The panic sent the deer into a running vault over the highway between two slowed semi-trucks. I felt the edge of the asphalt under my floorboard knowing the next few seconds would probably make or break my driving career. Would there be a ditch, a ravine, soft turf, a pond? Regardless, I wasn't dead yet.

The impact of the rough terrain change threw my trainer from his bunk and onto the floor. Behind me, I heard a terrified groan as his feet pounded the back of my seat with an empty thud.

"What the Hell?" he shrieked as the truck vibrated violently over the hardened earth beneath the steel frame. The trainer reached up and pulled the emergency air brake which brought the truck to an immediate stop. He looked at me with reddened bloodshot eyes and a quivering wrist from the shock of being woke up in the middle of a deep sleep.

Putting his face very close to mine, he yelled: "If you ever pull a stunt like that again, you're going to be walking back to Salt Lake!" Considering the circumstances, I felt he had let me off easy. "Now get this thing back on the road and I will try to come up with an explanation for why your left rear-view mirror is bent out of shape." I'm paraphrasing here, but I wanted to spare you the four-letter words. I think you get the gist of the conversation, minus the trucker lingo.

My hands were shaking; my heart was pounding, and my new-found confidence was crushed to a pulp. I knew I would not forget this day anytime soon and little did I know that this day would be the beginning of a new life for me. This was the day; the one that changes everything. When you are faced with death, somehow the stressed details of life seem less significant. The unpaid bills…the failing career…the marriage on the rocks all momentarily vanished in a haze of blue tire smoke. I found myself thinking about the life that was eroding away in front of my eyes as each mile slipped silently away, in the shadow the immense, eighteen-wheeler refrigerated box truck.

CHAPTER TWO

Morning Sky

REACHING INTO MY POCKET, I discovered a small handful of sunflower seeds I had nearly forgotten. Placing the seeds on my tongue, I could feel the gentle burning sensation of the salt crystals that flowed over the microscopic bristles of my tongue.

The sun was now just peaking over the eastern horizon carving vibrant colored images onto sparsely dispersed clouds between brilliant sparkling stars that seemed to promulgate into infinity. The brilliant red and gold colors that filled the morning sky with radiance was unparalleled in the vastness of this tiny planet. The blues and grays of the feathered clouds gave way to a piercing array of colors casting shadows over the hills into the dew fresh air, painting a canvas that looked like ghosts returning to their haze coated graves.

At last, the long semi-truck sat lifelessly along the roadside. I decided to take a break and watch the sunrise while I recovered from the driving fiasco that nearly cost me my life. The trainer had gone back to the bunk to get some shut-eye while I watched the line of trucks limp by. Drivers were seemingly grateful to be moving after the traffic jam that must have backed up for miles since our abrupt stop less than a half an hour ago. We had time to spare getting to Appleton so rather than jump behind the wheel and fight traffic; I sat down vagrantly on the soft dry grass that flowed out to a meadow for as far as the eye could see. You could barely see the tips of the buildings that made up the Milwaukee skyline less than twenty minutes away and it wouldn't be long before traffic would be stacking up in every direction. There would be no point in rushing now. Best to wait, because otherwise, the next few hours would be spent in bumper-to-bumper traffic all the way up along the shores of Lake Michigan.

I had seen many sunrises over the last seven weeks, but this one was unique. This sunrise had started me on a journey of deep introspection that would last more than four years and follow me over countless hills and valleys. The beauty of the sunrise caused a reflection within my mind; examining me both inside and out. What I would discover is that which was on the outside, would be just a shadow of the real discovery of what was happening inside; something was changing. I felt a modest glow inside; I will call it my God Box for lack of a better explanation because that is where the real miracle began that day.

CHAPTER THREE

Change of Seasons

APPLETON WAS A NICE TOWN, full of the things you would expect to see in a town of this size; like fancy bridges and historic buildings that keep the local culture fresh and alive. I'm sure I could talk up a storm about the history of this sensible little city, but I'm guessing you really want to hear about Elvis—I can't say I blame you. Nobody, it seems, is all that interested in a truck driver named Jeffrey, so let me tell you the story of how it all began. How Elvis became a part of my uneventful and frequently boring life.

"All you need to do is sign on the pages marked with a sticky tab," said the title specialist handing me and my wife a mound of papers across her long, makeshift desk. The signatures would finalize the bill-of-sale of our fashionable Vashon Island farm, just a short ferry ride across the bay from Seattle. This was our home; one we had worked hard to build over the last five years, sold in weeks to someone we had never met. The second large stack of papers would bridge our loans to our new home just south of British Columbia in the little historic Dutch town of Lynden, Washington. The documents would make me the temporary proud owner of more than a million dollars of real-estate, and although the power of ownership seemed glamorous at the time, the payments would soon dwindle our savings to nothing and our resources to zero, in less than a year.

After signing the inch-thick packet of documents, I didn't have to see red ink to know that I had signed a deal with the Devil himself. How the banks, the agents, the complex network of underwriters could pull all these financial manipulations off, was mesmerizing and I would soon find out that I was to become the victim of a global financial scam that would eventually circle the earth and bring the global financial markets to their knees.

To make a long story short, we lost everything, although we didn't file for bankruptcy until much later after trying to stay afloat for four agonizing years. We had lost a lifetime of investment and our family, my wife and three young children, wound up living in a custom-built designer home with no food in the cupboards except what my mother had gathered from the local food bank to keep us fed. Our fancy home would be sold at auction and my family and I wound up living in a mobile home park on the far side of my Dad's hometown; a neighborhood of petty theft criminals and recovering drug dealers, or so they say.

The degrees received from the same university my wife and I graduated from, now hung on the wall of a dimly lit trailer as a reminder of our decline into poverty. For months we watched our wealth drain away until the day I decided I would take the next paying job available, regardless of what it was. The next job just happened to be a trucking job. Within a few weeks, I found myself behind the wheel of a big eighteen-wheel semi-truck, headed for the open country. I was fueled with a new sense of pride that came with the job after having to jump through so many difficult hoops to gain licensing and then over the hurdles of getting used to driving a huge vehicle that had the capability of carrying a small regiment of smaller vehicles. The International truck that was assigned to me, drove more like a Cadillac than a truck, but so much more powerful. I certainly wasn't the King of Rock & Roll, but I was the King of the Road that year as I burned away thousands of miles from coast-to-coast with the wind in my hair and the memories of a broken economy in my tailwind. I felt alive and free again. The memories of my mistakes began to diminish over the next few years as I crossed some of the most desolate places on earth, while quietly relishing every wretched mile of it.

CHAPTER FOUR

Desert Oceans

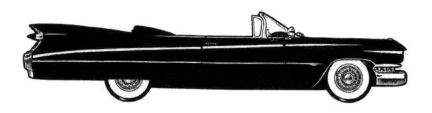

C ROSSING THE NEVADA DESERT, headed to El Paso was one of the most captivating stretches of land I had ever seen. Crystal blue salt lakes sparkled in the afternoon sunlight while the winds picked up in the afternoon causing a hazy fog, set just above the salt flats and mineral saturated crystal lakes. The brisk desert winds created blue and green waves over the surface that resembled an ocean paradise on the distant shores of a tranquil maritime mirage. It was heaven and hell blended as one in a subtle display of natural beauty; unless of course, you happened to be thirsty, or worse, crossing on foot. Recalling that very day, I sometimes think it might have been a mirage I saw, but I could swear I saw a long neck ostrich standing perfectly still in the foggy salt air feeding off the brine shrimp in one of the salt flats just a short distance from the highway. Brine shrimp were the only living thing that could survive the lunar-like landscape.

Anyway—where is this story going? Oh, I remember—you wanted to know how I became an Elvis tribute artist; of course. Over the last few years, many people have asked me that very question, and I think the answer can only be told in a lifetime of stories, but I'll try to spare you the details. In short, Elvis to me became an iconic part of a lengthy recovery process that was the result of some very bad financial decisions we made in the years, leading up to the Great Recession. Most of what we owned was sold or given away in less than a year. To take care of my family, I found myself on a long-haul truck traveling from coast to coast, twenty-four hours a day, seven days a week. The 'road' was a place of healing and I discovered a whole new side of myself that had been dormant under a layer of false belief systems and misguided priorities that, all that I believed was part of the American dream everybody should desire.

Only in troubled times do people ask the hard questions of life; for me, it was a long seven-year process. I pulled to the side of the road for a moment to see if I could catch a better glimpse of the ostrich standing perfectly still on the salt flats. It was about four feet tall and just barely visible from the highway. There were no inhabitants for many miles around these parts and I couldn't imagine how such a large bird could survive out here in the middle of nowhere. Where did he come from? Was he trying to find his lost mate? Did he have a family somewhere in the foothills along the flats? I found myself asking the same questions of myself. Much like the ostrich, I was a long way from home, away from the people that cared about me. I had become part of the landscape, just barely visible through the tinted glass of my red rig semi-truck. I had become nobody and felt every bit as alone and isolated as that strange bird looking for food and water in the desolate deserted salt flats.

That evening I pulled into a truck stop near El Paso. The evening was humid, yet comfortable, unlike the damp coolness of Washington State's climate I was most accustomed to, hundreds of miles to the north. Truckers, if you don't know, tell a lot of stories and I don't claim to know the truth behind most of them. However, there was one story I was told by an old trucker, late that night. A story I wouldn't soon forget. Even to this day, it was a doozy of a story…

"You look like Elvis," said a middle-aged man from the other end of the restaurant café bar. I had heard that a lot since I grew my sideburns out during my truck driving years. It wasn't really my intent to duplicate the King of Rock & Roll, but I thought the attention would add an interesting touch to my daily hauling routine; at least it would make for some very interesting conversation.

"Where you from?" he asked holding his cigarette just over the ashtray that was sitting on the long pastel countertop. His eyes and forehead were heavily wrinkled, his skin grayed, probably from the continuous smoking and driving hundreds over thousands of miles cross-country for too many years. By the look of his poorly kept gray-brown hair, I would say he was likely not married and was in his forties.

"Seattle," I said, sipping the freshly poured black coffee from the caffeine stained mug that had probably seen more miles than I had.

"I used to know Elvis," he said. "He was crazy—always goofin' off and pulling pranks. He was surely one of the friendliest guys I had ever met." Then he added, "Even though I hardly knew him; he acted like he had known me my whole life."

He paused suddenly, "Name's Jim," he said noticing he had managed to capitulate my interest. He slid casually down the bar to shake my hand. His nicotine-stained mustache all but covered his upper lip which fluttered as he spoke.

"Yeah, like I said, I knew the man—hung out at a few of his parties…seemed like he was having one about every weekend. I watched him hand the keys of a new Cadillac to one of his friends who needed a car. He had lots of money and he didn't' seem to mind sharing it with people, mostly old folks. He was really into that…you know, helpin' people less fortunate."

Listening to him talk, his story seemed to contradict the impression I had of Elvis which was more like that of a self-made vanity godhead. It has amazed me over the years how many different people I've talked to that all tell different parts of the Elvis story, that they would say the same thing about his down to earth personality. But, they liked him. Elvis seemed to make an impression everywhere he went and must have met a lot of people. The number of people he impacted in his life was astonishing and even today, his trail of fans encircles the globe, even after being dead for nearly 40 years. I knew if I could discover his secret, I would have a whole new chance at fulfilling my dream of becoming a professional singer. This curiosity took me on a parallel trail with Elvis across the country and my life as an entertainer would begin to shape over the next four years.

Jim appeared to be in an almost meditative state while he told his story about Elvis Presley.

"You know he was a truck driver for a time," he said. "Elvis drove a straight truck while he was working on his career in entertainment. Someone told me they were always telling Elvis not to quit his truck driving job because he probably wouldn't make it as a professional singer." I'm guessing that must have been a paradox for him because it seemed to provide the fuel he needed to keep going."

I thought of the many times people had told me the same thing. The odds of making it in the music business was difficult, even in the sixties. Encouragement is a hard thing to come by even for the most talented individuals. I wondered how many moments of doubt Elvis had to brush off and the tons of discouragement from his family members and even his closest friends he had to have endured.

Like Elvis, I had been in music all my life, beginning all the way back in grade school with the school orchestra. I took guitar lessons, but they proved too difficult for my parents to afford. Then, several years later I taught myself to the play the piano by ear. I discovered I had an uncanny ability to write music, but nothing would become of a lifetime of thankless practices and performances that yielded nothing more than an expensive hobby that gave me just enough false pride to keep me going. When I started driving truck, I thought I had left my music behind; then I discovered the Elvis Presley phenomena that was spreading across the country, especially in the southwest.

I was very curious about Elvis. I can't say I was much of an Elvis fan having grown up in the later golden years of Rock & Roll, emerging in the mid-seventies following Elvis's groundbreaking years. My generation of music was inspired by the works of Elton John, the Eagles, Willie Nelson and Paul McCartney to name a few. Having come from a conservative religious background; Elvis was the Las Vegas celebrity that turned his back on gospel music and the Church for a life of worldly pleasures and vain aspirations. I suppose a certain amount of that is true, but what I know about Elvis's private life, at least from the stories I've heard, is that he was just like everyone else. He was trying to make his way in a confusing world without a roadmap. Still, he had discovered the keys to unlocking the doors of fortune and fame that would forever inspire every artist that followed, including Michael Jackson, even to the present day. The Elvis phenomena continued to spread, and no one seemed to know why.

For me, my Elvis Tribute Artist career started out of curiosity more than anything else. I was five years old when my mother bought me my first vinyl forty-five record player—I was hooked. I spent the next thirty years of my life hoping to get on stage following the in the steps of the inspiring singer Elton John and his famous tune, "American Pie":

> *A long time ago*
> *I can still remember*
> *How that music used to make me smile*
> *And I knew that if I had one chance*
> *I could make those people dance*
> *And maybe they'd be happy for a while.*
>
> *Elton John*

These words had become my theme in life and I never thought the answer to my prayers would come from a most unlikely young fellow by the name of Elvis Presley.

CHAPTER FIVE

Legends

J IM AND I TALKED FOR QUITE A WHILE, sharing stories, most of which I have long since forgotten, but there was one amazing story that I truly enjoyed, -so$_2$ I hope you can indulge me for a moment and let me share Jim's incredible story with you:

"There is an old legend in truck driving that I'm guessing has been passed around over the years from truck driver to truck driver about a long-haul driving stunt that was done in the early seventies, long before the federal government stepped into micro-manage the trucking industry.

Truckers, as many as ten or twenty, would line up on the interstate bumper-to-bumper.

The truckers would all put their trucks in neutral except for the last trucker, who pushed the whole works down the highway with his rig. The front trucker then became the pilot so everyone else could take a break, eat lunch, or even take a short nap.

One trucker decided to finish a six pack of beer and in a drunken stupor decided to stand out on the doorstep of his truck to relieve himself. You can guess the rest. Going down that highway at over sixty miles per hour he lost his balance falling to the pavement leaving his truck unattended for the next twenty miles. It was probably the excessive beer that saved him from going into shock and he was discovered several hours later by his friend from an adjoining truck who figured out he was missing. They found him hunched over on a guardrail with several broken bones, a badly skinned shoulder, and a big grin on his face. I'm sure he was in a lot of pain, but he was alive—all three-hundred and twenty pounds of him.

Jim said he walked over and sat down next to him on the guardrail as curious vehicles slowed to examine the scene. The trucker appeared dazed and didn't speak; his bloodshot eyes only vaguely recognized his approaching friend who was there to help him. The first thing Jim noticed is that the truckers pant leg was ripped, and blood had saturated an area around his hip. Somehow though, his pocket radio was still intact. The old truck driver was nodding his head to a beat that was playing out loud since the headphones were no doubt mangled from the fall. 'You ain't nothin' but a Hound Dog', was playing clearly over the little AM radio. It would be several hours before emergency services would arrive so the two just sat and listened. What else could they do?"

Jim swore the story was true and unlike most trucker stories, he claimed he had been there and done it himself. I told Jim I thought that would be a good challenge for the television show *Myth Busters* to attempt. Jim and I shook hands and we parted ways.

My schedule had already come in for the next day on my onboard computer link. I was headed to Nashville, the home of the Grand Ole Opry. For whatever reason, Jim's story really stuck in my mind. Perhaps it felt like I was living the life of a cowboy in the wild west discovering the last frontier on American soil—or maybe, I felt accepted by the old timer, acceptance I so desperately needed during the difficult years that followed the recession. I had crossed over from another world and was experiencing a life that city folks probably wouldn't understand. I had uncovered a world I never knew existed and would never have understood unless I had experienced it first hand; the lonesome life of an over-the-road long-haul trucker.

I felt a sense of pride as I stepped back onto my big shiny red rig. I was alone and a long way from home, but I didn't feel that way tonight as I watched the faint glow of the sun disappear quietly over the horizon, west in the blazing El Paso desert sky.

CHAPTER SIX

Music Highway

I NTERSTATE 40 HIGHWAY, is a long hot stretch of
desolate road that would take me right up through the heart of
Tennessee past Graceland, Jackson, and several other towns
on the way to Nashville known as the Music Highway. I couldn't
drive through this part of the country without imagining the many
famous stars that passed through here—Johnny Cash, Merle

Haggard, Willie Nelson and literally thousands more traveled this road seeking fortune and fame in the town that represents the dreams of the many country music artists hoping to make *the big time*. Most of them would find a lot of very stiff competition in bars with other musicians who are willing to work for nothing to get their name carved into the legends of this historic city.

As I crossed the border into Tennessee, I reached up and flipped open the card my wife and kids had given me for my birthday the last time I was home which now seemed like over a month ago. The card pictured a photo of Elvis Presley taken live in 1974 at the Mid-South Coliseum in Memphis Tennessee. I happened to glance up and see my reflection in the rearview mirror and noticed that I was developing a strange resemblance to the photo on the birthday card. Even as my sideburns began to grow long, and my thick curly darkened hair smoothed out in the dry climate reflecting a light sheen in the bright sunlight, on both sides of my hairline. Already, people in the southern terminals were calling me Elvis for fun, but I never knew that these early driving years were about to take an abrupt detour that would so dramatically shape the next five years of my life.

As I stared with intrigue at the Elvis' birthday card, I couldn't help but wonder what it would be like to stand on stage wearing one of those incredible jumpsuits that must have cost a fortune even way back then. I knew that Elvis had them designed after his karate outfits, which gave him the agility to perform some of those spectacular blackbelt moves onstage during his performances. It added a real—excuse my pun— 'kick' to his legendary performances. My wife had also attached a family photo that slipped out and landed face-up in my lap. I was reminded of our daily arguments about finances, passing the blame back and forth while the kids retreated to their bedrooms to avoid the horrible negativity that seemed to perpetuate an already bad situation. I began to realize that I blamed everyone around me for the mistakes I knew I had made. Still, the photo reflected a perfectly happy family with all of us gathered together next to my big red diesel truck.

Everyone was smiling, and I wondered, "What had happened to the smiles? Was our situation so awful that it robbed us of our joy? We had lost our home, but a home is nothing without a family. Why couldn't our home just be us; me and my family, without all the 'stuff'?"

All my precious 'stuff' was at home—or gone. Living on the road for weeks at a time I rarely had carried than a suitcase full of belongings. Our losses had all but destroyed my relationship with my three kids and my marriage. My heart ached, and not just for me but for the many people around the world suffering quietly in similar circumstances. You couldn't drive through places like Phoenix Arizona and not feel the animosity of the families who had been devastated by the economic collapse in the mid-2000s.

* * *

I looked up ahead and saw a sign for the Casey Jones Museum just off the exit along the historic Music Highway. The name rang a bell remembering the song "Jackson" sung by Johnny Cash and June Carter, they recorded back in 1967. Although there was a long-standing debate over which "Jackson" the song was about, most music historians agreed it was most likely Jackson, Tennessee since it was the closest to Memphis where Johnny Cash recorded his first album at Sun Records.

As I set the birthday card down, I reached over and pushed in my 1974 Elvis Presley live concert CD into the player. The song, "How Great Thou Art" came on and I began to sing along as I often did on long drives to keep me awake and right now I was getting tired as evening approached. My mind creatively considered the images of my family still fresh in my mind from the photo and the strange connection of the Elvis' cover shot. Then I wondered how my life had gotten so far off course and couldn't imagine how it could ever be repaired. As the song echoed in the little chamber of the box truck:

> *"Oh Lord my God, when I in awesome wonder…", I began to feel the pain of life I had taken for granted. "…consider all, thy world thy hands hath made."*

The beauty of America I was experiencing was undeniable, and my problems seemed small in retrospect as I considered the vastness of the country many of us never truly get to see.

"Then I shall bow, in humble adoration..."

I thought of family arguments—trying to take control of a life that had spun hopelessly out of control and realized I could no longer fix it—my life was truly broken:

"... then there proclaim, my God how great thou art."

The rest of the song was sung with tears falling from my eyes as my wavering voice pushed a rush of air that passed gently over the delicate, now stressed ridges of my vocal chords from the sudden outburst of emotion.

It was somewhere along this very highway, the 'Music Highway', that my 'normal' priorities would begin to change and a new vision for my life would begin to take shape from one that had been lost along the dead-end pathways of greed and envy on which I had so carelessly and tragically fallen.

"Next Exit, Jackson, Tennessee home of the Famous Casey Jones Museum...

... Gifts, Food and Elvis souvenirs come join the fun."

I felt that endless pit in my stomach as if my stomach had eyes or something, and I decided to take a chance and see if I could find a place to park for the night. The next twenty-four hours would change my life forever and what better place to capture the moment and find a better road to travel than in Jackson, Tennessee at the very heart of the Interstate 40 Music Highway along Route 66, en route to Nashville.

CHAPTER SEVEN

Golden Rims

THE CASEY JONES MUSEUM, was one of the millions of over-advertised tourists stops plastered across miles of billboards that extended from coast to coast. You could pretty much plan your entire trip simply by watching the signs along the highway giving you the exact distance you were from the attraction, so you wouldn't miss the stop. Today, the internet and cell phones have all but outdated the necessity for large attractive entertaining billboards, but for me, they are great for keeping me awake during the long days and nights behind the wheel.

I have never been to an all Elvis store before but Jackson, Tennessee had one with all the legendary souvenirs you could imagine. The store was like its own museum with hundreds of photos and memorabilia hung on the walls anywhere a photo or a novelty could be placed.

I didn't grow up in the Elvis era but there was something about the historic photos of Elvis Presley that were captivating, especially the photos of Elvis and Pricilla. These images became the icons of their generation, almost too perfect to be real. If Pricilla changed her look, half the nation's young women would do the same making these two, the most sought-after couple in the history of marketing. Their photos were priceless and still are today.

As I studied the lengthy photo collection, I happened to catch a glimpse of the edge of a photo that was taken at Elvis' Memorial Service Broadcast on national television in 1977. Elvis was just 42 years old when he died. It seemed like an unfair tragedy that caused a tremor of loss that resonated around the world and continued to pass from generation to generation for at least 40 years and counting.

I pulled the photo out to get a better look. It brought back memories when I was fifteen years old watching our little Zenith black and white television with the curved tube screen and silver channel knobs. I, like most of the rest of the world, watched the Elvis memorial parade broadcast sitting together with my family on the sofa that faced the television. Dad wasn't much of a fan, so he thumbed through his flight magazine while Mom sat with a box of Kleenexes in one hand as tears streamed down her face. Her tears dripped onto the image of her 1958 'Movie Stars' magazine cover shot of Elvis, a magazine she had long kept concealed on the bottom of her sweater drawer for more than twenty years. The little droplets soaked into the magazine cover, rippling the delicate image that had shaped a generation. At fifteen years old I found it was difficult to understand the depth of sorrow she felt for someone she had never met. Dad reached down and grabbed the newspaper, skipping page one that featured Elvis Presley's full-page heading and photo that overnight reached nearly every household in the country announcing the tragedy. It puzzled me that Dad seemed uninterested in the event while Mom was having a difficult time hiding her embarrassment over the display of sorrow. I sat quietly glancing up only briefly trying not to focus on my mother's glossy blue eyes.

As the televised memorial procession continued in black and white, on the old tube television screen, I could clearly see the face of Elvis Presley lying peacefully in a large wooden coffin. It was not common, even in the late seventies to televise such a public display on national television. His face didn't seem real, certainly not the face of the unhealthy Elvis that appeared on national television in full stereo just two months earlier. His face was quiet and peaceful and his complexion perfect; much like the images from an earlier time before the Las Vegas lifestyle had taken its toll on his health.

The stories that would follow would be full of unanswered

questions and theories about his death; a mystery that would span decades in a search for the truth of which we may never know. A part of American history died that day leaving a generation of women widowed from a secret love affair that had lasted nearly twenty years to the day since the release of Elvis' epic recording, *"Jailhouse Rock", "Don't be Cruel", "Love Me Tender,"* and *"Won't You Be My Teddy Bear."* The instant fame these records delivered would begin to whittle their way through to the very heart and soul of Elvis himself until he became a prisoner of his own fame, locked in a cell of his own creation

I set the photo carefully back on the shelf in the little Elvis retail store as if it was part of a sacred museum collection. Out of the corner of my eye I spotted a small package of gold Elvis glasses sitting next to a few decorative Christmas ornaments on a series of glass shelves. The price for the cheap plastic replicas was just $3.99 which seemed like a fun novelty I could take home to remember this special place. At the check-out stand, I put the glasses on and asked the store owner what he thought. He appeared startled momentarily and did a double-take, squinting to make sure he was not seeing things.

"You look just like Elvis!" he said. Since he was the store owner, I was sure his opinion counted unless he was just trying to fluff up the sale. He held up a mirror and momentarily, even I thought I was seeing the image of King.

It was a simple cheap pair of TCB Elvis glasses, probably made in a sweat factory in China assembled by under-aged teens. I didn't want to admit it then, but these glasses had started a chain of events for me that would lead me to discover a new identity as an Elvis Tribute Artist singer and performer. The store owner asked a friend to take a photo of us together in front of his store. Little did I know, this photo was to be the first of thousands spread over social media, shared by countless parties, performances and appearances over the next five years and more.

From that day on, things began to change. I stepped up my voice self-training and began learning as much as I could about Elvis. I memorized as many songs as I could. Nearly everywhere I went in Tennessee, Alabama, Kentucky, Louisiana, and Georgia people would comment on how much I resembled Elvis.

Prior to my visit to Jackson Tennessee, people didn't notice me. Being a long-haul trucker gave me a real sense of pride in America, but it also made me feel that I was becoming invisible; a non-person.

I had become a faceless truck driver, a national pawn to be played by big execs in the name of trade and profits; part of a hidden infrastructure that most people didn't even know existed.

In densely populated urban areas, people stop at the stores daily, pick up fresh produce, meat and their choice of literally thousands of coffee flavors; ground, whole bean, espresso brewed to their liking. It turns out that it isn't politicians that make America great every day, it's the American long-haul trucker—the most thankless unrecognized force on the planet. They come from all walks of life for all different reasons; some for adventure, some for financial reasons, and even some just needing a place to live. It is said that at any time you can line up a days' worth of rigs on Interstate 80 Highway and stretch them bumper to bumper clear across the United States. After sitting through a few traffic jams, I believe it is true— but I'm guessing, you would probably rather hear about Nashville.

I pulled into the Grand Ole Opry parking lot about mid-afternoon. The parking lot was attached to a large shopping mall that was being gutted for remodeling due to a flood that had passed through the area the year before. My timing was perfect for getting in to see a show as well as enough time to spend a few hours at the Grand Ole Opry Hotel.

Entering the old theater, I had the same anxious feeling that kids feel, walking into Disneyland for the first time. This was the center of country music for the entire country and you could almost feel the heartbeat of the nation pumping through the veins of countless radio stations, records stores, and AM/FM radios that were networked together twenty-four hours a day, seven days a week.

At the epicenter of this modern metropolis, was a little circular wooden stage patch that was originally cut from the original Grand Ole Opry, still standing in Nashville at the time the new theater was built. As I sat forward in my seat carefully examining the stage, I could just make out the edges of this incredible piece of American history. Nearly every famous honky-tonk, bluegrass, crooner, early rock 'n' roll, and county star had stood on that very spot to sing at one time or another. They stood at the center of the stage marked by a very rugged, carefully preserved piece of aged, old-oak flooring that had survived fire damage, water damage and countless music style changes for nearly a century.

As the lights dimmed, a commercial would be played out on stage because the show was still broadcast live over the radio, even to this day. At the end of the commercial, the announcer queued Ms. Sarah Cannon, better known as Minnie Pearl. Her stage act was no less than the work of genius. In an instant, she captured the hearts of the entire audience as she had done for more than 50 years.

"Howw-deeeee!" she belted out lifting her hand to her ear in anticipation of the spellbound audience's loud gratuitous reply as we all responded, "Howww-dee."

If there has ever been a historic human relic in the flesh, it was Minnie Pearl and here she was in full 3D true-to-life color. She was soon followed by Little Jimmy Dickens and I do mean 'little'. At just under five feet in height, he put on an incredible show at age ninety; one of the oldest living legends of country music and old radio comedy in the history of the business.

Somewhere in the mesmerizing climate of the historic center of county music, just as the carefully coordinated stage lights began to dim, moments before the next stage performance was to be announced by the legendary Jimmy Dickens; something welled up in me from deep within. Something strange and wonderful began to move in me like a slow stagnate river closing in on the rapids, carving their way through a steep shadowy canyon in a dense rainforest. For the first time, I realized that I wasn't like everyone else. I was different. I belonged on that stage up there with Jimmy Dickens and Minnie Pearl. I discovered my deepest passion was to become an entertainer, to be one of the many talented individuals that gave people a moment of happiness and peace into their mundane daily lives.

I remembered my mother's tears dripping down on the pages of an old magazine. As I looked down away from the stage I could see the same teardrop impressions on the printed program in my hand creating a ripple down the page that crossed a small historic photo of Elvis Presley towards the bottom. I didn't know how I would ever pull it off or what it would take, but I wanted to be on that stage; whatever it takes, I wanted to get there.

Music has always been part of my life, but it was always overshadowed by the practical discouragement of family and relatives who, like Elvis, didn't think it was a good idea to quit my day job. I reflected on the many years of performances with bad recordings, lean recording equipment and more than fifty original songs that had yielded absolutely nothing. My elaborate speaker system and collection of guitars were gathering dust and age, yet I couldn't bring myself to sell them in the hopes I would be inspired to take another stab at my music career.

I grabbed a tissue and wiped away the next teardrop trying to hide my embarrassment. The show was supposed to be funny, but my tears were not about the years of failure I had experienced in music, but rather of joy as I began to understand that creating music was not all about money, success, CD sales, or commercial contracts. It's about stepping into a parallel world that is outside ourselves, opening the deep caverns of our lives that hide the secrets of life—the joy, the peace, the freedom, the passion, and all things that move us forward and makes life worth living. The heart of music is not just a place, it's inside all of us and we can drown it out so easily with traffic noise, cell phones, credit card bills and family squabbles. Music never ceases—it's always there. I had almost forgotten the gifts God had given me and it took thousands of miles over hot tar and gravel packed roads to bring me to this very turning point.

While the next commercial aired on the national airways from that little theater just outside of downtown Nashville, I tipped my head and said a little prayer. It wasn't a big profoundly worded prayer with lots of creative old English adverbs; "thee's" and "thou's", but rather a simple prayer—a promise if you will; that if I ever had the chance at life again outside of trucking, I would spend more time with my family and I would learn to sing Elvis songs like nobody's business, God willing… and yes, I kept that promise.

There was no lightning bolt, no hallelujah chorus, no blessing from the Pope; but there was a moment of loud clapping as Minnie Pearl again stepped onto the stage for a few more laughs, but somewhere across the room in an unnamed empty seat, I could swear, I heard an angel clapping just for me.

The pre-programmed wireless spotlight once again beamed down on the little stage cutout as if God himself was saying, "This is where you belong, but you need to learn to trust me first—and by the way, you can't park your semi-box truck in the parking lot of the Grand Ole Opry overnight—better get moving." Okay, maybe I am paraphrasing that second part, but to this day, I am still trying to work my way onto that historic stage. It sounds crazy, but the next four years of my life have been nothing less than that, pure crazy and sweetly wonderful!

CHAPTER EIGHT

Dixieland

DRIVING THROUGH THE HEART OF VIRGINIA, on highways that cut through the beautiful landscape that was once used mostly for farming, I noticed the commuter traffic beginning to pick up considerably. The cars looked new and expensive; not what you would expect out in the middle of nowhere. I'm guessing the land was now mostly owned by wealthy city workers, lawmakers and bureaucrats, purchased more for the quality of the views and the lifestyle, rather than agriculture. This was such a strange demographic, being this far from a major city;

even a city as big as Washington D.C.

"Oh, I Wish I was in the land of cotton, old times they are not forgotten, look away, look away, look away Dixieland..."

These were the words being sung by Elvis from his 1972 rendition of a classic combination of American inspirational and patriotic songs. I remembered Elvis singing this song live on television in his 1973 concert "Aloha from Hawaii."

I punched my new coordinates into the GPS that would take me right through the heart of Dixieland and onto Warsaw, Virginia; a little town with less than 1,500 people just south of Washington D.C. My truck's governed timeclock was nearly up which meant I wouldn't have enough hours to continue driving beyond Warsaw. I would have to stop.

"Washington D.C.", I thought to myself. I have always wanted to see the monuments of Washington D.C., but getting in there with a fully loaded semi wasn't going to be a possibility and I was out of driving hours. So, the next morning, I caught a commuter train that took me right to the heart of this amazing city.

Even before arriving at the station, I felt there was something very powerful about this region and you could feel it in every bone of your body. Many of the nation's smartest people were located here on a narrow tract of land that didn't belong to a state, but instead, was originally donated to the people of the United States by Maryland and Virginia to build the most important structures of our nation. They named this small tract of land, the District of Columbia.

The federal buildings were impressive. Even from the train, I could see they were built to last. Stepping off the train, I knew I would be seeing our nation's Capital on foot and my aching feet would only acquiesce the feeling of enormity that I felt most of the day.

I spent hours browsing the museums that were all free to the public. As I rounded the corner walking around the south side of the White House, I looked across the massive campus and caught my first glimpse of the National Monument. It was grand; even from a distance. This was truly an incredible life moment that changes your life forever. I felt a sense of history, conflict, energy, and power as I gazed at the magnitude of the National Monument and the surrounding structures. The day would be perfect if I could just get to that monument and place my hand against the smooth white marble and granite face of this magnificent structure.

I walked along the concrete pools that led toward the National Monument, now completely empty for some reason. Thoughts of the recession rebounded in my mind as I passed along these historic ponds that I had seen in so many historic photographs. Now they appeared empty, dirty, and lifeless, without geese, fish, or any wildlife to frolic in the cool waters that once mirrored the heavens.

The walk to the National Monument was surprisingly distant, deceptive due to the ancient Greek architecture; it was much further than it looked. I reached the circular grassy region around the monument, taking a moment to sit and marvel the grandeur and size of the inspiring, man-made structure. After a moment I stood and stretched my legs and started my quest, so I could place my hand gently on the side of this great symbol of our nation.

It turned out to be more symbolic than I thought. There was a wire fence all around the base with signs warning visitors to keep out. Some of the granite was pulling loose so access to the monument was cut-off.

"How ironic," I said to myself. Three thousand miles from home in the heartbeat of America and I see a sign that says, "Don't touch." I suppose I could spend hours talking about the symbolism of recent presidents that have squelched the voice of Americans, who are isolating themselves behind the safety of these grand structures and the politicians insulating themselves from the true voice of Americans. Standing less than thirty feet from this grand symbol it occurred to me that Americans were accepting these "Don't touch" policies that had been feeding corruption as the power of the people quietly dwindles away.

How far we had come from what our forefathers envisioned that our nation would be "a government of the people, for the people, by the people". When did we become a nation of minority thinkers and a nation that is under lots of gods, other than a nation built under the God that forged our great nation?

As I stepped away from the steel-mesh barrier that separated me from placing my hands on the National Monument, it occurred to me that we all need to start taking more responsibility for what goes on behind these walls. Welcoming socialism into our government was a stab in the back for the people who died to preserve the nation's freedom. I could no longer place the blame on media, the gridlocked Congress, or the overpaid lobbyists. I realized that the blame for our nation's problems lied squarely on my shoulders and that I needed to start taking more responsibility to save what is left of our freedom.

I headed down the path toward the Lincoln Memorial then onto the Veterans Memorial Wall. It was here that the words of 'American Trilogy' in 1973, sung brilliantly by Elvis, sunk in:

> *"Hush now little baby, don't you cry. Your daddy is bound to die."*

I placed my hand against the long smooth black granite with the name of our veterans who had died for our nation. I could almost hear their voices screaming out from their graves that they wanted to be remembered and that their deaths would not be in vain. I thought of the hundreds of thousands of service-men and women across the nation that were suffering from the lack of proper medical treatment, inadequate funds to support their injuries, apathy toward their needs and limited counseling for their families. Just because we choose not to think about our problems; doesn't make them go away.

As I took the stage in Dallas Texas at the South Fork Ranch, where Larry Hagman had brought to life the fictional character J.R. Ewing in the television drama, 'Dallas', I looked over at the crowd through the blinding spotlights and foggy red, white, and blue neon lamps that beamed eagerly through crowd. I remembered that moment as I walked along that big black granite wall humming to myself:

"Oh, I wish I was in Dixie, away, away... in Dixieland I'll take my stand, to live and die in Dixie."

I held my right hand high in the air as if I was holding an American flag in a battle against ignorance and neglect. Then I spoke these words while the band played the instrumental segment of the song. Getting down on one knee I said, "We can no longer live as a divided nation. We don't need more liberals or conservatives fighting over front-page media space. What we need is more Americans willing to fight for our freedom and our constitution so that our veterans will not suffer in vain. This is the greatest nation on Earth, but it cannot thrive on division. So please join me right now in bringing our country back together and let this next chorus be your voice in unifying our broken nation."

In that moment, I heard the harmonic voices of the backup singers chiming in over the powerful high-fi sound system. Then the drums started playing what sounded like 'The Battle Hymn of the Republic," a battle march ensemble leading into a triumphant symphony of percussion instrumentation. The lights of the stage lit up like torches as the keyboard player and the base and guitarist dug into their instruments as the crowd sang:

"Glory, glory, hallelujah. Glory, glory, hallelujah. Glory glory, hallelujah. His truth is marching on."

I held the final note until I was breathless. Then I heard a thunderous applause from the crowd and for the first time, I got a small taste of what Elvis must have felt singing over national television for hundreds of thousands of people from all walks of life; all around the world. In that patriotic moment, I envisioned the empty pools leading to the National Monument refilling; a moment of true patriotism that made this country strong. It's a message that is long overdue and one we need to revisit soon before it is too late. I stepped off the stage, remembering everything in my life that had brought me to this place and the freedoms that allowed me to be whoever I wanted to be; a telecommunications specialist, a manufacturer, a trucker, a builder, a publisher and my favorite; an Elvis Tribute Artist. We live in a truly great nation. Let us never forget!

CHAPTER NINE

Florence

BOARDING THE COMMUTER TRAIN, that would take me back to Warsaw Virginia that evening, I caught a brief and final glimpse of D.C. in the distance as we journeyed down the clicking rails, down past Alexandria and several other small towns I had never seen. As I climbed back onto my big rig I could hear my onboard terminal already beaming my next mission from a satellite high above the Earth. Florence, Alabama would be my next stop along the road.

Florence was at the very heart of a region that might have inspired Elvis. Nashville was straight due north from Florence and Memphis was due west. The Tennessee River flows west, northwest from Florence through Memphis where it joins the Mississippi River then heads south to New Orleans where Elvis filmed one of my favorite movies in 1958, "King Creole". The film opens with a vocal duet on the streets of New Orleans with southern black American singers that capture the heart and flavor of this historic steamboat town. The song "Hard Headed Women" became another #1 hit on the Billboard pop charts. Elvis managed to capture the heart of this wonderful region with its long humid days, warm breezes, and the smell of shrimp Creole.

"Got one!" I yelled as the tip of my fishing pole dipped violently, catching me by surprise; the live minnow I was using for bait had worked like a champ. I reared back to set the hook, but having never fished these parts, I didn't have a clue as to what kind of fish might be on the end of the pole, if a fish at all. Whatever it was, it was big.

I smiled at the younger middle-aged black man fishing just a short distance from me down the old wooden plank dock. I had struck up a conversation with him earlier and he had told me he was unemployed. I surmised he was fishing for more reasons than sport, he was feeding his family. When you live in poverty for a time like we did during the recession, it always helps to talk to folks that have it worse than you, as a reminder that God manages to take care of all of us; sometimes in very unsuspecting ways.

The black man's eyes perked up. He could see my big red rig a short distance away and was amazed that an outsider had taken to the local fishing spot with such finesse—truth be told, so was I. I had made some very quick friends at the fishing shop just hours earlier because I looked like Elvis. They were more than willing to share all their fishing secrets to make sure the King caught a fish.

The fish jerked and headed toward the open waterway. I watched my line start spinning off the wheel like a runaway top. If I tightened the drag, the line would snap. If I let it run, the line would run out and the fish would slip away with the line, hook and the unlucky little minnow in its mouth. I wasn't about to let this one go. Because of its size, I knew I wasn't going to be able to land this fish, even if I did get it close to the dock.

The fish jetted sideways toward the rocks and I could feel my line skipping on the large jagged rocks that were hidden just under the surface. The fish must have intuitively known he could use the rocks to cut my line. Immediately I lunged off the dock into the rocky shallow water. I sank up to my waist, all to the amazement of the black man a short distance away, now hurrying to reel in his line, so he wouldn't hook me, or worse, get his line tangled in mine.

The fish's plan to snap my line on the rocks didn't work, so he decided to make a run toward open water. The river was as vast and deep as you could imagine with massive sandstone cliffs on either side. At that moment, the fish, no doubt, had the homecourt advantage.

My reel spun loose and popped clean off the drag nut. I tried to grab it before it sunk to the bottom beneath my feet; I missed, just as the black plastic line spool jumped off the real and headed for open water along with the fish leading the way. The remaining line zipped through my pole, and like a long toy slinky; it then rested on the surface tension of the vast body of water. I used a few catchy fishing words that I'm sure grandma wouldn't have approved of and threw my pole down to let it sink to the bottom. Then an amazing thing happened. The line stopped moving. It just sat there floating on the surface in a long spindly mess, but the fish was still on!

"Get the line!" yelled the black guy from the dock. I didn't hesitate. Ripping off my shirt, I dove for the line that was now slipping slowly beneath the surface.

"Got it!" I yelled in a splash of victory as my head popped up above the surface. The fish was worn out from the fight and so was I, reeling him in like a long extension cord. It was a largemouth bass; a common fish in these parts. It was at least ten pounds, but I didn't have a scale handy to weigh it, so I can't say for sure exactly how much the fish weighed—okay, maybe it was a couple pounds but a nice fish nonetheless. I had no way to clean it or cook it, so I handed it to the black fisherman, with a twinkle of pride on my face. He smiled as if he had caught the fish himself.

His family would be in for a nice treat that night in these hard times. My black friend had a small fish feast for dinner that night, along with a great fishing story to tell his kids.

THE GOD BOX

CHAPTER TEN

Gators

MY NEXT DELIVERY, would take me deep into the heart of alligator country to a small city called Ocala, Florida. From there I planned to drop my trailer and head for the nearest sandy beach. The Northwest weather that year, along with the depressed economy had been particularly bad, so I looked forward to getting a little vitamin D into my system. To avoid the expensive tollbooth charges, west towards the Atlantic Ocean near Fort Lauderdale, I decided to head east instead towards Yankeetown Florida. I should have studied my geography harder before making the two-hour trek because the only beaches there are alligator mud slicks and a lot of no swimming signs posted by the tourist stops along the lagoon.

I was driving toward Yankeetown headed for the mouth of the Withlacoochee River when I noticed a road sign that read, "Elvis Presley spent July and August of 1961 in this area filming his ninth major motion picture, "Follow That Dream". I once heard that the filming for this movie was done next to the Bird Creek Bridge, but I was hard-pressed to make out any resemblance of today's beach in comparison to the tropical wonderland portrayed in the movie. I guess Elvis couldn't find a sandy beach here either, so he had one brought in for the filming. The beautiful white sands in the movie have all but vanished leaving nothing more than a mud slick pull-out for tourists to dump their trash. Here they could catch a glimpse of a dream that now exists, only on a steel reel of a carefully stored film, somewhere in a private collector's home in Hollywood. The film reached #5 and became the top-grossing film in 1962. Today you might be more likely to get your leg bit off by an alligator than catch a fish off an old bamboo pole.

I managed to find a bar-restaurant that had a big gravel strip for me to park my big rig. I don't know if Elvis actually ate at that particular restaurant in the 1960's during the filming, but it is now completely remodeled with a tiki bar on one side where patrons can sing karaoke on the weekends. Today happened to be a karaoke day and the place was already filling with tourists and locals for the occasion. People were already curious about the fact that I looked like Elvis and they were hoping I would hang around and sing. I was curious as well and enjoyed suddenly getting more attention than I was used to.

I picked a song that I thought I knew but as it turned out I didn't, so I just followed the keys and the prompter and hoped I wouldn't embarrass myself. I had never sung Elvis songs in public since I started driving long-haul, but I wasn't about to the let the audience down. They had more confidence in me than I did in myself.

Then I sang as the old gospel piano tune started:

"As the storms of life are raging, stand by me."

Elvis arranged and recorded 'Stand by Me' in 1966, a song that became one of his greatest gospel hits:

"As the storms of life are raging, stand by me. When the world is tossing me, like a ship out on the sea. Thou who rules wind and water, stand by me."

When I finished singing, I dipped my head hiding my embarrassment from the crowd, but a strange thing happened; they loved it and they didn't even seem to mind that I wasn't familiar with the tune. For them, I had brought Elvis back to life right off that phony white sand beach just a few miles away, and for a moment, you could almost feel the wind blowing through the coconut palms that extended down the beach to water. Something wonderful happened to me that day and that song would become the theme song for my life as I began to work through the difficulties of repairing my marriage and rebuilding my relationship with God. This was the furthest I would ever get from my home, but it was here, I discovered a gift and an answer to prayer. God had given me a voice to bring joy into the hearts and souls of all who hear it in the years that followed.

In 1961, Elvis and the movie crew packed up their belongings and hit the road. In 2008, I simply turned the key that powered up my big red International truck, popped the clutch jolting the rig from side to side as the huge tires gripped the asphalt with immense power beneath my feet.

It was back to Ocala to pick up my refrigerator box trailer, then I would head north up the Interstate-75 Highway. Then it was onto Bowling Green Kentucky, such a strange name for a town. I was delivering a load of Florida oranges before loading up again to head for the west coast down Interstate 40 over what was left of Route 66, in the golden years of Elvis Presley.

CHAPTER ELEVEN

Elvis Country

CROSSING THE BORDER ON I-65, headed north to the little town of Bowling Green, Kentucky, I thought I would commemorate the crossing with a song on my "Elvis Country" CD, which now slid gently into place under a complex laser system, that instantly detected the audio tracks. I pushed the fast-forward button until a familiar song I had sung many times along the road, played loudly through the truck's door speakers, drowning out some of the noise produced by the powerful Detroit diesel engine, churning at an arm's length away beneath the long, extended cab hood.

"Seven lonely days, and a dozen towns ago,

I reached out, one night and you were gone.

Don't know why you'd run, what you're running to or from,

all I know is, I want to bring you home.

Kentucky Rain keeps pouring down."

The Kentucky rain is no joke. I found the Pilot truck stop I was looking for, where I could refill my tanks and maybe spend the night. It was there I spotted a young man in his thirties hitchhiking from the entrance of the fuel depot. He was protecting his head from the heavy rain with a trucker magazine, now saturated, providing little shelter from the torrential Kentucky downpour. It was hard to make out his features as the wipers imperceptibly swiped away the heavy flow of rain and hail pelting against the large, fragile International truck windshield. I was just a short distance away from the terminal where I would drop a trailer and pick up another load before my required overnight driving break.

As luck would have it, this was a fully decked out Pilot that even included a little theater for watching movies at night. I grabbed a healthy meal of fruit, nuts and a thirty-two-ounce Coke to wash it down with as well as trucker size hotdog with all the condiments; cheese, chilly, onions and every kind of sauce you could think of.

I'm sure my wife wouldn't have approved. I could swear I heard her faint scream three thousand miles away in the back of my mind.

I managed to drip some of the mustard on my over worn, wrinkled short sleeve shirt. As I reached down to wipe the spot off with my napkin, I noticed a bulge around my waist that was once trim and fit from the years I had spent in construction back home. Out of sheer guilt, I set the candy bar down that I held tightly in my other hand but couldn't bring myself to let go of that hot dog, not today. Everyone has their weaknesses, mine was hotdogs.

That night on the theater big screen TV, they played an old Elvis movie released in the 1960s called, "It Feels So Right." During the haunted house scene, Elvis throws "Pam", the girl of his dreams, over his shoulder in a sudden cloud burst of rain and lightning.

From across the dimly lit Pilot theater, I could see a younger man sitting with a clenched grip on a damp trucker magazine he had been using to protect himself in the rain outside while trying to hitchhike. From the looks of it, he wasn't having much luck.

As the actors found refuge from the storm on the small white screen, I remembered our vacation to Chattanooga Kentucky in 1988. We had only been married a few years and already we were experiencing the burden of finances in the economic downturn from the oil boom of the early 80s in Oklahoma City.

My wife and I had just had a big fight in our hotel room and she had walked out slamming the door behind her. It was a few minutes before I followed. The Kentucky rain and thunder outside no doubt was drenching her tightknit sweater, ruining her expensive high heel shoes. My anger burned, and yet at the same time, I was beginning to feel concerned that she might not be coming back. I walked around the huge hotel complex for over fifteen minutes before finding her tucked in the seat of our white, hardtop Cadillac sedan.

Immediately, I ran over and opened the door allowing the pouring rain to drench what was left of her rain-soaked outfit. Her hair was matted with moisture and her makeup strewn down her eyes with a mixture of tears and rain, dripping on the soft leather seats. She looked up at me, then grabbed the door handle and yanked it closed with a healthy tug. The door managed to catch my head in the upper window nearly knocking me unconscious. In what could only have been a knee-jerk reaction, I ripped the door back open and reared back to kick her in the leg—I missed. She was bent over slightly in the seat and my bull-hide leather boot landed smack dab on her cheekbone causing a little bloody cut that seeped into the mixture of rain and tears.

I realized in the moment that I was becoming a monster, the same arrogant jerk I vowed I would never become. I stepped back slowly and humbly, shutting the door behind me. Sitting down on the cold wet pavement, I dipped my head in shame. It had all been an accident and yet there was no excuse to cover my actions for what had just happened.

My wife didn't leave me that day, but for a time, the romance of our early youthful marriage had come to an end. As the event faded into the distance it was replaced with a more permanent bonding of love, one that looks past our mistakes and heals all wounds. For the next thirty years and counting, there would be many trials and hardships, but I would never forget that cold sleepless night in the pouring rain at that big lonely Kentucky backroads hotel.

The words of the song Kentucky Rain still looped in my head sitting in Pilot's little theater as we watched the classic Elvis movie. Quietly visiting with my new hitchhiker friend, the soundtrack played on in the background:

> *"So I finally hitched a ride from a preacher man who asked, where you bound on such a cold dark afternoon? As we drove on through the rain, he listened, I explained, and he said a prayer, that I'd find you... Kentucky Rain keeps pouring down..."*

The rain-soaked hitchhiker had made one last attempt to hitch a ride outside on the road. He finally returned to dry off and watch the rest of the movie. As Henry was eating a few of the free sample products from the Pilot truck stop store, I figured he must be broke and hungry. That was a feeling I knew all too well; still, something stood out about this young man as a mysterious inner voice began to tug at me.

"There is something for you to do," the voice said.

"Not tonight," I said to myself as I gathered my belongings and headed back to the truck for a long, quiet night's sleep—alone once again.

THE GOD BOX

CHAPTER TWELVE

Hitchhiker

I WAS OVERCAUTIOUSLY PETRIFIED, staring at the large stack of papers across the long narrow desk in front of me, in an empty office with bland walls, no pictures and coffee stains on the floor.

"Just sign here," said the Vashon title officer handing me a large stack of papers, all tabbed and organized for my wife and me to sign.

A simple signature would sign away the rights to our beautiful private Vashon Island farm across the bay from downtown Seattle and give us the keys for our new custom home in Lynden, Washington, located two hours north, just below the Canadian Border.

My hand shook nervously as I pressed the pen to the page. I wasn't sure why we made the decision to move, but I would have the next ten years to think about it. When I arrived back at our three-acre farm, we discovered that one of our alpacas had died. We learned it was probably caused by some poisonous weed that had sprung up in the pasture, in the hot, dry summer.

Then, it hit me. I gazed around the beautiful private property of the small island ranch that had become a home for my growing family over the course of just five years. We had worked so hard to build this place. I looked down the hundreds of feet of fencing I had installed by hand; Nancy's garden, the sheds, and a beautiful red barn. It had truly become a piece of paradise. In less than a week, we would only be allowed back here as guests on the property.

I laid down on the soft pasture grass next to 'Pepper', our black Alpaca and began to weep, gripping the ground as if I was trying to hold onto the land I had so thoughtlessly signed away a few hours earlier. As I turned my head sideways, I looked straight into the blackened glazed eyes of the dead Alpaca; his tongue was hanging to one side and I could just make out a tiny dried teardrop, stuck to one of his lifeless eyelids.

"God—I'm sorry!" I yelled at the top of my lungs. I sat up and hit my head on the upper bunk inside my big red semi. It was a nightmare, one of many I would have on the road. I could hear the early truckers starting their engines getting first dibs on the long stretch of diesel pumps that extended outward from the *Pilot*. I pulled the privacy curtain back, and there was that same hitchhiker, standing out on the sidewalk trying to find someone to drive him to Hollywood California.

My days started pretty much the same. The first hour of the day I usually spent waiting for my onboard computer to tell me my break time was over, so I could get back on the road. The hitchhiker had come into the restaurant and was eating crackers he had picked up from the salad bar, I was sure he hoped no one would notice.

"Have you eaten anything?" I asked the young man just a short distance away. I could hear the crumple of cracker rappers in his pocket crinkling as he looked up in embarrassment. He was about my height and it looked like he had not shaved in a few days.

"I'm just fine," he said, fidgeting nervously as if he had just stolen something of value, "—why do you ask?"

"You've been here since yesterday, and by the size of the crumpled wad of cracker rappers you have there in your pocket, I'm guessing you haven't had much to eat either."

"Henry Downer is the name," he said reaching out politely with a hand, partially coated with crumbs. "My trucking company went bankrupt and left me stranded here."

"Where's home?" I asked.

"Hollywood," he said.

"Gees, you are a long way from home," I said.

"The company left me to fend for myself and locked my company credit card down as well. I'm guessing I won't see that thousand-dollar paycheck either. What a scam," he said, tipping his head in shame. "—I can't believe I fell for it."

With that off his chest, he reached up and removed his hat, carefully adjusting the band and placing it back over his brown, grease matted hair.

I watched him for a moment then said, "Here's my Pilot card and ten bucks. There's a free shower on the card and enough money to get a Subway sandwich. That should tide you over," I said, flashing him a quick smile, smugly proud of myself for a good deed for the day, or so I thought.

"Thank you, sir," he said shoving the card and the crisp dollar bills into his damp pocket, still slowly drying from the relentless rain that could still be seen in the parking lot, just outside the glass entrance doors.

I still had an hour before I was able to leave the terminal, so I spent the time listening to the radio while I waited for the little green indicator light to pop up on my dashboard truck terminal.

I tuned into one of the Kentucky AM stations, it was a Nashville talk show host that was playing the intro of 'Guitar Man' recorded by Elvis:

"Well, I quit my job down at the car wash, left my mama a goodbye note. By sundown, I'd left Kingston, with my guitar under my coat.

I hitchhiked all the way down to Memphis, got a room at the YMCA, for the next three weeks I went huntin' them nights, just lookin' for a place to play.

Well, I thought my pickin' would set 'em on fire, but nobody wanted to hire a guitar man."

I grabbed my beat-up guitar from the top bunk inside the semi cabin and started picking out the chords to the song. As I sang along with the radio, I couldn't get Henry Downer out of my mind. I'm sure by now he had plenty to eat and was cleaned up. He was probably on a ride down I-40 already, headed towards Memphis. Still, that voice nagged me and wouldn't let go as the green light flickered on my terminal giving me the signal break time was over.

"Okay God," I said to myself. "I'll drive around the truck stop once. If he is still standing on that sidewalk looking for a ride—I will pick him up—deal?" I continued in my thoughts, looking upward as if to see an angel smiling down at me from heaven. Instead, I noticed that the top of my windshield was heavily caked with bugs from the damp humid southern Kentucky drive.

I locked my GPS into Inglewood California, a town just south of Los Angeles. This load would take me down the Interstate-40 Highway. This stretch of highway extended all the way from Raleigh, North Carolina to Barstow, California. The new four-lane Interstate highway dwarfed the original ~~route~~Route 66 that used to run cross-country down through Oklahoma City during the Great

Depression. The old route, took travelers across some of the most desolate terrain on the planet, heading westward approaching the desert oasis of beautiful Southern California. Today it is difficult to trace the old highway, but many people make the attempt each year for old times' sake. Today, a Model-T Ford would do well to avoid this highspeed roadway during rush hour altogether.

"Henry," I yelled out the side window catching the young hitchhiker quite by surprise. "—hop in."

Looking a little stunned, he came around the passenger side and jumped into the seldom-used cab bucket seat. His hair was still damp from a fresh shower and his face and clothes were freshly groomed. The crinkled cracker rappers in his pocket were replaced with the remaining half of his foot-long deli sandwich.

"Thanks, man… thank you so much," he said.

"Well, you can thank my trucking company for giving me a load all the way to Hollywood."

"You're taking me all the way to Hollywood?" he said, lit up with a sudden glimmer of hope in his eyes.

I gulped before responding, realizing I was committing the next three days to someone I had never met. Maybe he was a bank robber, had killed someone; maybe he was on the run. I would never know, nor did I want to.

"Did anyone ever say you look like Elvis?" he said, noticing the acoustic guitar I had tucked behind my seat.

"I get that a lot these days," I said, responding with a grin.

"Right-on—TCB—yea, I'm a big fan…you could pass for the King," he said, and I wondered why he was a fan of an entertainer that had been deceased before he was born.

I wasn't much of big fan having grown up in the seventies in the Great Northwest far from the influences that made Elvis a folk hero, but I was always surprised by the dedication of the fans that I met across the country, especially in the southern states. Elvis must have really been a special individual. He somehow managed to touch nearly every household across the nation for better or worse in one form or another. This ability was intriguing, and I spent many hours of drive time pondering how he did it.

Was it his great looks, his charisma, his dancing, guitar playing, his fancy cars and pink Cadillac's or something much deeper? Something we have missed, just out of sight? If I could figure it out, it would certainly help my music career which was for the moment—in the tank.

I slipped the gear shift into high gear and it glided in smoothly, feeling much more confident that I was beginning to master the technique. Henry and I were headed south through Tupelo Mississippi; the birthplace of Elvis Presley. There I would pick up a load of frozen fish, then we would head back up through Memphis, home of Sun Records where Elvis did some of his most famous recordings. It was there that a man named Sam Phillips would steer Elvis away from the gospel his mother loved and the music he had grown up with. The more than thirty original gospel recordings Elvis made in Memphis would never be released to the public, even to this day. There was no need for old gospel tunes any longer as the rising superstar entered the mainstream of popular blues and the radical new sounds of the rock & roll era that made him famous.

CHAPTER THIRTEEN

Memphis Gospel Legend

TURNING MY TRUCK WESTWARD, heading into Memphis along the I-40, I reached up and pulled down a shrink-wrapped compact disk, clipped to the sun visor. It contained a collection of Elvis' gospel songs that would help me relax from the stress of the busy traffic going through Memphis.

My favorite was the gospel song, 'I Believe.' It is one of several Elvis gospels that managed to survive his transition to the new era of fancy hip movements and rubber leg stage dancing that pushed his records to the top of the charts in less than a year. For me, it was less than four years after driving that truck across the country that I would sing this very song before a live audience in Las Vegas, to a large crowd of eager Elvis fans.

"Yeaaah! Jeffrey 'Elvis' Fullner," yelled the announcer to the crowd at the 2016 Elvis Tribute Show being held at Sam's Club in Las Vegas. It was my first time on stage with a touring national band, complete with powerful backup singers, a horn section and the versatile sounds of the industry's best guitarist, keyboard players, and bass guitarists that I had ever had the privilege of performing with. My blood was pumping through my veins, captivating the spellbound Elvis fans as I sang 'Burnin Love'.

After my first song, I got a moment of rest backstage before my second song, while another Elvis Tribute Artist took the stage. I had never been backstage before during a concert, but it was one place I can't say I enjoyed spending a lot of time. The other singers were stressed and on-edge, rethinking every word of their performance; prepping their voices using these god-awful sounds and drinking water like radiator fluid on a mid-day desert road.

One artist really got my attention. He had the best and classiest jumpsuit that money could buy. His hair was perfect and so were his sideburns; both looked authentic—although I'm guessing, they were ordered online from some online Elvis accessories supply store or some other place. He was pacing nervously through the interconnected dressing rooms, taking moments to breathe and sip more water to keep his vocal chords moist and acute. He stopped for a moment in the middle of the room and I watched his eyes close. His hands tipped outward as he began to pray. This was not the vain Las Vegas-style image I expected to see and certainly not the gaudy projection of the Elvis my parents warned against over dinner when I was a child. This was a humble man, making his way in the world just like me. For the first time, I wondered if any of what was said about Elvis's vulgar lifestyle was true. Perhaps it was all a front for a much gentler, friendlier Elvis that few people really got to know, in the long narrow halls of the backstage. Maybe Elvis was more than just a highly paid commodity for marketing companies to exploit while launching their latest products on the national airways. Perhaps in the dimly lit quietness of the restricted backstage changing areas, he was a person who had forfeited his privacy and given up his stake in the simple life. The real Elvis must have been left behind in Graceland. Maybe in that lonely, anxiety packed space, he was just like me.

Stepping back onstage with a more humbled demeanor as the band started the introduction for my song, "I Believe", I noticed the song started slightly off-kilter as if the band wasn't sure how it was supposed to begin. The off-beat tone threw my concentration and I found myself struggling to remember the words. I started singing a mixture of verse one and two together which was setting the stage for certain disaster going into verse two.

God must have heard my frustration. Suddenly the stage lights went black and the crowd of more than four hundred people vanished in darkness in front of me. The instruments in the band stopped abruptly as the amplifiers, speakers, equalizers and countless dollars of equipment shut down instantly. I stood there in complete darkness waiting for something—anything to happen. The entire casino power grid had dropped, and it would be at least five minutes before the systems could be brought back up.

In the darkness of the now quieted and confused theater, the announcer lit up a small lighter that lit up the corner of the stage. The panic of the crowd eased as the little fragile light flickered. Then I remembered the road that brought me here. It had hardly been four years now, driving that big red box truck cross country, listening intently to the story of the passenger whose life would never be the same, on the long ride from Kentucky to California along the old Route 66

It was there that I remembered my quest, and that my god is the god of second chances; today I would have mine. Returning to the now brightly lit stage a short time later, I gave a stunning performance the audience would not soon forget:

"I believe for every drop of rain that falls, a flower grows..."
"I believe that somewhere in the darkest night a candle glows..."

"I believe for everyone who goes astray, someone will come to show the way..."

"I believe...I believe."

I wasn't the only one who had become a believer that day, and I had no doubt that God had his own agenda going on in the backdoors of that busy casino; a demonstration that made an impression on myself and the audience. A least at that moment in the dark silence of the packed theater, I was a believer—I think we were all believers that night!

CHAPTER FOURTEEN

D EEP IN MY THOUGHTS, I couldn't help but stare at the empty road behind me; a long stretch of interstate that seemed to roll right up into the horizon.

"I'm an atheist," said the traveler sitting just a few feet away with a mouth full of chips from the bag I handed him from behind the seat. He must have heard me singing under my breath, one of the Elvis gospel songs I had loaded on my CD player. The outburst caught me a little off guard and I wasn't sure how to respond.

Growing up in the church, I wasn't sure I knew exactly what an atheist was. Most people believed in God to some degree or another but here was someone who did not. Standing outside in a Kentucky rain downpour would make any man rethink his religion. I had spent enough time around the Pentecostal Church to know that when you are walking with God; or in the *Spirit;* as they say, a lot of what some people call coincidence really does begin to happen.

It was the stories of how God's presence in people's lives is what drew me to the church early on. It wasn't until many years later that I discovered that Elvis was raised in the Pentecostal Assemblies of God Church as well. It was there he learned to sing and dance, but it's also where lines were drawn that would step him onto his own path, leading him far away from his traditional Christian roots. This is where the paths of Elvis and I cross and the similarities in our discoveries would take us down many roads, many of which would turn out to be dead-ends; often sounding good on the surface at first but lead nowhere.

"You're not going to try and convert me are you Jeffrey?" Henry said as he finished the bag of barbeque chips he was eating and wadded it up, carelessly dropping the bag on the floor I worked so hard to keep clean each day. I assumed he meant converting him to Christianity.

I watched the last of the billboards disappear behind me in the distance; huge advertisements for tourist stops in the historic

Memphis downtown where Elvis had built his fame and fortune. I too was curious about Elvis' beliefs. The fact that he had died at such an early age of forty-two, gave me an uncomfortable feeling about his intrigue with spiritualism; a path that may have led him away from his biblical faith.

"Well Henry, I'm not sure I have a roadmap for that," I bantered back. "I'm only taking you as far as Hollywood. Heaven is a lot further."

He laughed detecting the play on words, but it would only be the beginning of a long and introspective discussion we would have.

I'm not a biblical expert and I'm sure that if God wanted this guy converted to Christianity he would have chosen someone else for the job. It wouldn't take me long to come up with at least ten reasons why I won't be going to heaven and I could think of only one reason that has made me believe I might make it.

"I grew up in the church. I was there until high school," he said shifting ever so slightly in his seat. "The preacher at our church was an evil man. His face would burn with fire on Sunday morning yelling at the top of his lungs that Satan would destroy me if I continued sinning. At the age of twelve, I had stolen a pack of chewing gum then made the mistake of telling my parents. They, in turn, told the preacher and the rest is pretty much what you'd guess. The next Sunday he walked right down the aisle and pointed that great big finger right in my face and told me I was going to hell unless I repented. Fear gripped me deeply as it did most of the kids my age although none of us had an opportunity to talk about it much; for us, we were just like any other kids; we just didn't know any better."

Henry had kind of drifted off into his own little world as he shared his life's story in surprisingly intimate detail for someone I had never met.

As we crossed the bridge into West Memphis, we could see the mighty Mississippi and what a spectacle it was. The sun beamed down on the wide crossing that must have been an intimidating sight for the earlier pioneers who had to cross the river by riverboat. For us in the truck, it would be a thirty-second crossing before continuing west toward Little Rock, Arkansas.

"So as an atheist, you don't believe in life after death?" I said curiously.

"Of course not," he snapped back. "When you are dead you are just dead. That's why we got to get what we can get while we are alive because that's all there is—there's nothin' else for you!" he snarled as he adjusted the heavy green backpack between his legs.

It didn't look to me that he was getting much of anything, and I was beginning to wonder if everything he owned was stuffed into that worn out green backpack. "What a hopeless point of view," I thought to myself.

"So, is that how atheists view the world?" I said out loud. "How hopeless is that?" I added.

"You see, there you go again, trying to convert me. Everyone is always trying to convert me," he said.

His atheist convictions weren't very convincing, and I could tell the hardness of his heart was beginning to leak with guilt. There was something about me and those wonderful Elvis gospel tunes that were setting him on edge as if being confronted by his own confused self-wired theology.

"Christians are only good at one thing", he interjected. "That's making other's feel guilty while they wade in their own hypocritical crap. I remember this clergy member in our church in L.A. that claimed he was a *born-again* Christian that everyone was excited about. One day he cornered one of my Sunday School classmates in the church office and tried to molest her. He might have gotten away with it had the pastor's wife not walked into the room carrying a big batch of homemade cookies, unaware of the drama that was unfolding in front of her very eyes. She didn't have a clue as to what was really going on, but those of us in the Sunday school, we knew. The next week when the pastor was out of town; the clergy member was asked to preach. That kind of did it for me."

I wasn't in the least bit surprised by his story and the rejection of the church that followed at such an early age. I had heard these stories all too often over the years and had even experienced similar incidents; church members that would dress to the nines on Sunday, only to discover a completely different person under the surface during the week. I'm not suggesting that dressing sharp for church on Sunday is a bad idea, but I think it can become a false coating for the truth about their failing marriages, their broken homes, and the real reason they tip their heads low during the long service prayer time. When the pastor asks the crowd if anyone has a prayer request, the church is silent.

My prayer has always been the same. "Please God; help these people stop working so hard to hide their sins. It isn't working very well for them."

"We have all had experiences like yours in church," I responded. "I have had my run-ins with church hypocrisy many times, but I think the thing to keep in mind is, churches are made of people, and when you have people, you have real problems. The Bible says that Jesus didn't come to save the righteous, he came to save the sick and at least in my experience the church is full of them. God reaches out to each person in a different and unique way. Granted church people get a little judgmental at times but then we all do. It's wrong but it's natural to shun people that aren't on the same page as you and may not share your beliefs."

I popped the twist top off my soda and took a drink as the afternoon heat was bearing down on the giant refrigeration unit attached to a trailer I was hauling. The unit was running overtime trying to keep the load cool for the long trip.

Finishing my thought, I said, "The truth is, God's relationship with us can't be judged by the way he relates to others. Our relationship with God is unique and it's up to us to trust in him every step of the way. Christians can be just as much of an obstacle to growing in faith as non-Christians."

"Tell me about it," he said. At last, there was a connection. As the city lamps and busy city life began to dissipate behind us, I realized we had reached a point of agreement. I think some of the larger church denominations deify biblical figures, but I often wonder what life was really like for Jesus, having to put up with twelve disciples. I'm sure they had many challenging moments during their travels. According to the Bible, they were all too human, or so it would seem.

"If God is so great, why would he let innocent people die and good people suffer," he said. "I mean look at me, I had to stand out in the rain all night trying to hitch a ride from a truck stop because some idiot boss at my trucking company decided to walk off with all the cash, leaving me stranded in the middle of nowhere?"

"Are you a good person?" I asked.

He paused for a moment as if losing his train of thought. "Well no, but that's beside the point. I've done lots of things I shouldn't have done in my life and this isn't about me, it's about those righteous church hypocrites."

"That's exactly the point. The Bible says no one is good, not even the pastor. We have all fallen short and we are all destined to pay an eternal penalty for things we have done in our lives."

"Yea, that clergy guy that attacked my friend, he's going to hell for sure," he said.

"I thought you were an atheist," I shot back.

"I am!" he insisted.

"Atheists don't believe in heaven and hell," I said, "and besides, you don't know where that guy was at in his relationship with God. Don't you think God is working in his life the same way he is working on yours? How would you feel if he was the judge of your life and declared that you were going to hell?"

It's funny how we all look at things from our own perspective. As much as I've tried to see things from God's point of view, I just can't. Most of what I see each day doesn't make any sense to me. The most important Bible verse that has kept popping up time and time again in my lifetime is Isaiah 55:8 that reads:

"My thoughts are nothing like your thoughts, and my ways are far beyond anything you could imagine," says the Lord.

"The Bible says that *Hell,* is a place where people have weeping and gnashing of teeth. Have you ever ground your teeth together until they bled? Of course, you haven't but this is precisely the description that Jesus gave in his sermons over 2000 years ago. Would you ever wish someone to go there? If it were true, wouldn't you want everyone to avoid going to such an awful place? Wouldn't you want to stand on a street corner and yell for people to follow Jesus if you knew they were destined for such a place? I know I would.

Young Henry Downer had heard enough and couldn't think up a response that would sway me towards his way of thinking. The sudden transition from truck driver to over-the-road evangelical preacher was probably a little much for the young man at that moment, so he grabbed a small dirty pillow out of his pack, pressed it up against the window and fell sound asleep.

His dreams would be troubling; I could tell by his lip movements and expressions while he slept. If God was speaking to this man in a unique way, this was surely it. Two thousand miles across country in a box truck loaded with thirty thousand pounds of fish scraps headed for a dog food packaging plant with a guy that looks like Elvis; how much more evangelism do you need? Hallelujah and pass the sunflower seeds. We were in for a long journey.

THE GOD BOX

CHAPTER FIFTEEN

FROM MEMPHIS, we headed due west through the heart of Arkansas towards a little town called Little Rock. As we drove through, my dispatcher called and asked us if we could reroute up to Joplin, Missouri to swap loads with another truck that was hauling a time-sensitive Walmart shipment to L.A.

I looked at Henry and he said, "That's a long way out of the way."

"I don't have to be home anytime soon. Go for it."

I took my headset off, which immediately ended the call and popped in one of my classic collections of Elvis songs. From I-40, I caught a glimpse of the Arkansas River as we passed through Little Rock. An old track of Elvis recorded live in 1956 at the Robinson

Memorial Auditorium, Arkansas played over the little dashboard speakers. The crowds of screaming women could clearly be heard in the background, drowning out the iconic voice of Elvis at times.

"I've got a woman, way cross town; she's good to me oh, yeah.

Say, I've got a woman, way across town, she's good to me

oh, yeah…"

There was something about Elvis' voice in the 1950s that was unique, and as an Elvis Tribute artist, I've yet to hear it duplicated. I could only imagine the wild performance that took place there sixty years earlier; a stark contrast to the polite mannered, humble young man that carved a new notch into the archives of music history.

CHAPTER SIXTEEN

Back Hills

I DECIDED TO TAKE A DETOUR, and see a little of the Arkansas, backcountry which probably would have cost me my job had my dispatcher found out. We got off the main highway I-49 and took the alternate route north along Highway 71.

Having not spent a great deal of time in Arkansas, I could not have known how difficult it would be navigating the windy backwoods mountainous regions. At one point the road narrowed so much, I nearly hit a school bus going in the opposite direction. The unsuspecting bus driver nearly had a heart attack as we rounded a sharp hairpin turn at the same time going opposite directions.

It surprised me how remote this area seemed from the rest of the world. I drove through town after town of homes and vehicles that looked pretty much the way you would imagine. I could almost hear the backwoods echo of the guitar and the banjo in the movie "Deliverance," as we rolled along the old highway.

Just then a song came on the cab AM radio. There wasn't much worth listening too way out here, but the old-style gospel was apparently alive and well in these wooded hills.

In 1974, a singer named J.D. Sumner recorded an old gospel tune 'live' with Elvis Presley in Memphis, Tennessee. J.D.'s deep bass voice was so low it vibrated the speakers on the dashboard. I turned up the song about halfway and tried to sing along, but I didn't remember the words even though I heard it many times growing up sitting next to my grandma in the little Reformed Church I grew up in.

"Try me, Lord, if you think there's a way, I can try to repay all I've taken from you.

Maybe Lord, I can show someone else, what I've been through myself,

On my way back to you,
Lord help me Jesus, I wasted it so help me Jesus,

I know what I am..."

The song sunk deep into my soul as I imagined what Elvis must have felt singing along with such talent in those years in the little town called Memphis.

Somewhere along the road north of Winslow, Arkansas, we stopped to take a break. My legs were killing me from the constant shifting and slow windy driving. The turnout had a trail that led down to a small river that extended deep in the Arkansas Mountains. Henry was also getting weary of the long drive but followed along peacefully.

A short distance away, a middle-aged man had quite a contraption laid out on the beach and he was using a long suction hose to draw sand from the creek bed. Upon further inspection, I saw that he was using a small dredge system to pan for gold. I had heard about the gold in Arkansas but figured it was all hype to sell elaborate gold panning machines to the next generation of entrepreneurial gold diggers.

"How's the gold panning today?" I yelled over the hissing and grinding of the fancy machine. He reached up and shut the pump off.

"Good. It is really good actually."

His response came as a surprise. "You mean that thing actually works?"

"Sure," he said but you got to know where to pan. You see, just over that hill is an old mine where gold was discovered years ago, and the gold deposits were good. After the price of gold fell, the mine was shut down." He reached down to show me the sifting mechanism and sure enough, it was covered with gold flakes. "You see?" he said smugly.

Henry wasn't the least bit interested. He lit up another cigarette as he walked further down the beach.

"How much is that little bit of gold worth?" I asked.

"About a hundred bucks", he said. Only took me six hours today.

"Panning like that could give a man gold fever," I joked.

Exactly . . . you see, most people look down the river and just see sand and dirt. For gold panning, we see opportunity at every curve of the river where the water slows down and the gold comes to rest.

I could just barely see Henry in the distance as he neared the first bend in the river. I thought about the miles of river I had seen over the course of the last two years and never once considered the possibility of finding gold there. The river and Henry seemed to become one in the distance as he disappeared in the rocks and the thick river overgrowth. There must be something I could tell him; some catchy piece of wisdom I could use to help get him on a path leading back to God instead of away. Knowing that I had my own struggles and doubts as a believer, would make it impossible to try and convince him there was a God that could save him. Hours of arguing theology and sharing beliefs had yielded nothing other than he had obviously read more books than I had.

However, for some strange reason, I felt that God had given me a revelation that day. Maybe, I was so engrossed in the sand and dirt of life that I couldn't see the gold just beneath the surface. I was very well read on many subjects but felt helpless against the cultural shift towards *relativism* that was plaguing our culture, creating an endless pursuit of self-indulgence, steering us carelessly away from the biblical truths that could save us. Henry was a piece of work, but as he turned around to head back towards me I could see the golden reflection of the sun reflecting off the water that sparkled around him. There was a weakness in his prideful philosophy, but I couldn't put my finger on it. Perhaps there was a weakness where pure gold had not yet been discovered, but one that God knew was there all along.

CHAPTER SEVENTEEN

The Storms of Life

WE ROLLED INTO JOPLIN, late that night and decided to spend the night in the Walmart parking lot. My head hit the pillow on the lower rear bunk and I would be asleep in minutes. Henry refused to sleep on the top bunk, so he rolled up his pillow for padding against the passenger side window and slept in the seat.

That night I awoke to the sound of complete silence. There wasn't a single sound except the occasional rumbling of distant thunder. It was so dark I couldn't see my hands in front of my face. There was no light coming from any direction and I figured I had either woken up in Hell or I was in the darkest place on Earth. I felt around for the dome light but in the darkness, I couldn't find it. A hint of fear began to grip me.

I found the lamp, but the bulb wouldn't come on which meant the truck battery was probably dead. Then I peeked through the privacy blinds to finding that my onboard satellite terminal was also dead. Henry must have gone for a walk because he was nowhere to be found. There were no street lights except for a red flashing stoplight that was running on reserve power. Even the Walmart store behind us was completely dark with a few of the emergency battery powered lights just visible through the windows as I stepped out of the truck to see if I could spot Henry. I thought it was strange that even his pack was missing and the sandwich wrapper he had left on the floor was gone. Maybe he had left during the night to catch another ride to L.A.

The sky was brilliant. I could see every star clearly and I was even able to make out the rings of Saturn and some of the cloudy details of the vast sea of stars that make up the Milky Way. Even the all-night signs from the fast food restaurants were turned off and there were no signs of life anywhere.

In the distance to the west of us, I could see a mammoth cloud formation that flashed constantly with sharp bursts of white light temporarily blinding out some of the stars above it. Between flashes you could see the massive cloudburst pressing upward like a giant nuclear blast, only this one circled as the extreme variations in barometric pressure vaulted the dense, humid vapor high into the atmosphere.

It was warm and balmy for such a late-night hour and I could feel the gentle gusts of wind beginning to whisk through my sleep-matted hair and the fragrant smell of summer rain beginning to fill the air.

In the distance, just beyond a large dumpster, something moved. It was a large dark shadow and it was clearly moving. I yelled out "Henry!" but there was no response, and yet the shadow kept moving and pausing momentarily near a strip of overgrown grass next to the highway.

I ran towards it see what it was. It appeared to be a large black animal that looked like a horse but with different features. As I got closer, the creature looked up with a mouthful of damp moist grass it was chewing on with long slender teeth that resembled that of a camel. It was an Alpaca of all things, a black one whose features I could just make out against the darkness of the night. It looked like *Pepper*; but what would an Alpaca be doing in the Walmart parking lot at night? I tapped myself on the side of the head to make sure I wasn't dreaming and stepped forward to see if I could get a closer look. The large animal was spooked and tipped his head up. His eyes must have picked up a flicker of light from one of the nearby emergency lights because they suddenly burned bright red, then he quickly turned and scampered briskly off into the darkness.

The storm was growing rapidly as it gained momentum and got closer. As the sun began to light the western sky, the enormity of the cloud formation was coming into view. The worst of my fears were beginning to unfold as the tornado sirens began to sound all around the town. In the wee hours of the morning, very few people would have been able to hear the warning sounds, and many would perish that night if they didn't seek shelter. It was a reality I knew all too well from having spent my childhood years living in the path of 'Tornado Alley,' in the northwest corner of Oklahoma City.

The winds picked up and I began to feel tiny droplets of rain across my face, I knew would turn to a thunderous roar in minutes. I decided to discontinue my search for Henry and head back to the semi. The red color of the large box truck cabin was just becoming visible as the sun lit the eastern sky, but I knew the dead battery was going to be a challenge for me.

I tried to call emergency road-site-services to come and give me a jump, but my cell service was not working. All of this was very strange as my fears began to escalate and turn to panic. The cloud that was approaching was no ordinary cloud and I was beginning to hear what sounded like a distant train coming into a train station. The good news was that I had parked my truck facing the storm which would improve my chances of survival should the storm produce high winds; or worse, a tornado.

I sat in the driver's seat quietly trying to find anything that worked but even the radio was dead, still no sign of Henry. The winds picked up violently minutes later as torrents of rain and hail slammed against the windshield. The truck began to sway violently, and I could see objects beginning to move outside in the rapidly increasing wind and rain. The storm whisked across the large parking lot like a dust storm on the desert floor and it was then I realized that I was on the edge of what must have been a very large tornado.

Tree branches and debris whizzed by the truck and large hale slammed against the windshield causing cracks and pits to appear everywhere. I could only imagine the terror of young families waking in their homes in the surrounding areas to the sound of shards of broken glass and broken timbers beating against their houses. In the dense cloudy rain that filled the morning sky, I could see several of the Walmart do-it-yourself sheds lift off the ground, rolling across the parking lot. The truck was now jerking and shifting violently in every direction and I had no doubt it was going to roll over. I was trapped; there was no place to go. In the rear-view mirror, I could see that even some of the roofing of the giant Walmart warehouse was beginning to pull loose.

The small do-it-yourself shed rolled and broke apart into a mass of blowing sheet metal and it was headed straight for the truck. I jumped into the lower bunk behind me hoping I would be safe from the impact. The broken shed rolled and tumbled and finally lifted for one last catapulting vault into the air before smashing into the front of my truck. The steel trusses of the shed smashed out my front window exposing the cab to the now violent forces of the high winds and rain. The golf ball size hail ran sideways into the rig hitting me like shotgun shells. The last heavy gust of wind threw me to the side window of the little cabin as the entire truck rolled over in an instant screech of grinding metal and frozen fish guts.

I yelled out at the top of my lungs, "I'm sorry God, I made a mistake, please forgive me, give me another chance!"

Then I heard Henry yelling from somewhere in the darkness, obviously terrified from the commotion.

"Wake up!" he yelled gripping my shoulders on both sides and shaking me. "You're having a dream. It's just a dream—Wake up!"

The distance between reality and dreams has always been a mystery to me. In confusing times, dreams can take on a reality of their own, but we remember them as if they were real. I sat up and hit my head once again on the top bunk. The inside dome light was now on and I could hear the hustle and bustle of the early morning traffic along the highway. Already, early birds were coming into work at the Walmart store and construction workers were starting their work on the completion of the new parking lot.

I was still fully dressed from the night before and my hair was sleep-matted.

"You were yelling!" said Henry. "You woke me up—gave me

quite a stir."

"You heard that?" I asked. "What did I say?"

"Something about a black Alpaca," he said. "You said you used to have one of those on your farm."

In the haze of the bright morning sunlight piercing through the window, I realized the strange black animal in my dream, must have been *Pepper*, my Alpaca that we had on our farm on Vashon Island that died several years earlier. I never really shook the guilt from allowing the animal to die and I wondered if the financial breakdown that came later, was somehow tied to the untimely death of this peaceful creature.

"Thank you, Henry. Sorry about that," I said still working on trying to regain my senses after that incredibly realistic nightmare. I stepped out of the rig after checking my terminal to find everything as it should be except for several small details. In the distance over-looking a valley, I spotted a long tree line over a half-mile away. There were many trees and homes to the north of us, but there was none in this area in either direction. The trees over the neighborhoods in the west also looked odd. The trees had all been cut back to their main trunks and left with only limited branches and leaves.

It finally hit me where we were. We were in the middle of what had been the epicenter of one of the largest tornadoes to strike a populated area in U.S. history. This was the restoration zone of a very large tornado that destroyed most of this small town and left a strip of devastation spread over more than a mile wide. The Walmart behind us had been moved back several hundred yards from the original location that once stood right where my semi was parked.

Henry joined me outside carrying a thermos of cold coffee he had pulled from his backpack. His leftover half lit cigarette filled the fresh morning air with the dull flavor of tobacco.

"People died here!" I said as Henry approached. I must have looked like I was in a trance.

"I know," he said. "We are in the middle of what must have looked like a war zone a year ago," he said. "I saw the video on TV. It even made the headline news in L.A."

"Life is so unpredictable, and death can come so unexpectedly," I said. "These people weren't warned. They never knew what hit them. Their lives and dreams were shattered in an instant and many of them died," I continued as if thinking out loud. "The horrors of those who survived must have been worse than death while family members spent weeks searching for their belongings on streets they couldn't even recognize. Children, pets, family photographs—you name it—scattered over a fifty-mile radius." Henry looked at me with deep concern as I rambled on.

In the distance, you could hear saws and nail guns echoing over the empty valley as residence rebuilt their livelihood in the small community.

"Are you ready?" I asked Henry.

"Am I ready for what—to get back to L.A.?", he said, confused by the pointed question.

"Are you ready to die?" I asked again.

"When you're dead you're dead. There's nothing else—you're just dead," he said flicking the remaining ashes of his cigarette on the pavement leaving a dusty patch of white cancerous debris on the freshly paved blacktop.

"Without Jesus, we have no hope. These people lost everything. What is their hope? Why rebuild when a storm can crush you in an instant?" I asked staring into his eyes.

"Jesus should have been around to save these people's homes," he muttered. "I think he let them down... such a waste." They didn't deserve what they got; especially all those helpless kids".

"That's exactly my point," he continued. "Jesus didn't save anyone—I mean look at it. It's just one big nothin' as far you can see in every direction. I saw on the news that even a big church took a hit. Where was God in that? Maybe a few members were cheatin' on their offering plate donations that week. Maybe God is as fed up with people as I am. They are all gullible and varying shades of stupid. I think their religion suits them perfectly," he scoffed finishing his broken speech with a shrug of his shoulders.

For once I didn't have a good comeback for Henry. He had hit the core of the matter smack dab in the middle. I'm sure one of the midnight T.V. preachers would have a good comeback for his statement, but not me. All I could think about was the beaming red eyes of the black Alpaca in my dream, how they seemed to look right through me to the depths of my own guilt and shame that I had been carrying with me like a boat anchor over thousands of miles of interstate for nearly two years.

"Maybe you're right," I said to Henry. "Maybe there is no God," I said wiping the rest of the sleep from my eyes.

"Well I wouldn't go that far," said Henry, sensing his statement might have pushed the discussion a little too far. "I didn't say there wasn't a God."

"I thought you were an atheist," I said looking him squarely in the eye.

If he was indeed a true atheist, his atheism was weakening. The view over the empty, desolate valley that once was lined with beautiful trees, stores and homes had obviously affected him. He was no longer convinced himself he was right. I think he was backing off because, in some way, he may have been jealous of my faith and my hope that had carried me this far. I think he knew I had something he didn't, and all these pointless arguments yielded only one thing, that he was searching for something to hold onto; something he must have missed along the way on the long windy road of his complex and disjointed life.

"Breakfast?" I said, smiling as he ground his cigarette on the asphalt beneath his dusty boots.

"Yeah."

The McDonald's restaurant golden arches gleamed bright yellow on the outside wall of the newly constructed Walmart store.

"Now Open for Business," the large banner read.

"Let's go for it!" I said.

"Amen to that," he said, assuming I would be paying since we both knew he didn't have a single dime on him.

CHAPTER EIGHTEEN

Royal Blue

I N 1972, Elvis took the stage in Madison Square Gardens in
New York City—the *Big Apple*. It was his first visit since the
1950s. His live recording went triple-platinum making it one
of the most successful recordings of his career. The royal blue
jumpsuit with the symbol of the owl on the belt buckle sparkled and
lit the night sky.

"Well I've never been to Spain, but I kinda like the music.

Say the ladies are insane there, and they sure know how to use it.

They don't abuse it, never gonna lose it.

I can't refuse it.

"Do you have everything," asked Winnie-Lynn walking around the sides of our big 1982 Ford LTD 4-door Station Wagon. The long yellow hood housed Ford's big block engine that would easily make the long trip to Seattle, Washington where I would look for work in the computer industry. The sides of the station wagon were trimmed out with wood-grained panels, the last of a dying breed.

"Yes, Mom," said Nancy-Anne, rolling her eyes. "I have checked everything twice?"

Nancy and I had only been married a short time but already, the Oklahoma City economy was not good in 1987 and the high-tech industry had not yet caught up with the west coast where jobs were booming.

"Do you need some more snacks for the road?" she said, examining the large brown sack of food she gave us the night before.

"Momma—you got us a ton of stuff last night. Our car is full and we're only going to be on the road for three days."

"You might get stuck somewhere for a few days?" she said.

"—We'll be fine," Nancy-Anne interrupted.

Winnie-Lynn hesitated for a moment. It was as if the reality of her blonde, blue-eyed little girl moving away for good was beginning to sink in. Her face turned red and I knew she was trying to force back the tears. Her husband Jimmy-Charles was standing at a distance, straight-faced, unsure why we had decided to move so far away.

"I think it's the right thing, Momma—God told me so," said Nancy-Anne with a courageous smile, wiping away a tear that had worked its way down her cheek.

I reached up and shook Jimmy's hand. It was firm, but I sensed his loss. Nancy-Anne was their golden child and she had never been more than a day's drive away from home in her whole life. The next few days would take her far away and they would not see her again for over a year. It would be years before I would understand the feelings her parents felt that day. It wasn't until I had my own daughter that I realized the bond parents share with their children.

As we pulled away from the curb, I watched Winnie wipe away a few more tears and Jimmy-Charles waved never once changing his expression. He was a good man, one I would grow to respect over the years. The house disappeared into the midst of a long cloud of dust, kicked up by the tires on the narrow dirt road that led to the highway along the tall, dried summer grass that extended to the horizon in every direction. Our world had become much bigger that day, but I will never forget those last moments, as long as I live.

"Henry!" I said, reaching to grab my cowboy hat from behind the seat of my big red semi-truck. "Turn up that song," I said. "Elvis is on the FM radio." We were just twenty miles from the Oklahoma border, and we were heading west through Tulsa and on to Oklahoma City. We stopped that night and had dinner with Nancy-Anne's folks. It was there I was once again reminded of the difficult decision we made to leave nearly thirty years earlier.

"Why did you leave Oklahoma?" asked Henry once again prying open the discussion that would no doubt take us to the next state line.

"That's really none of your business," I replied, trying to change the subject.

"Let's see," he paused. "—you were broke, your marriage was on the rocks, and you and your wife lost your jobs a day apart from each other," he said, repeating the full story back for me.

"So how does that work? You said God provides all your needs and that he takes care of the least of his creatures on the earth. From what I can tell, your needs weren't being met at the time and you were worried you would be out on the street if you hung around any longer. I know it's none of my business, but it looks like God doesn't always provide for our needs; at least in your case," he said scooping up a mouth full of sunflowers seeds to offset his craving for a cigarette.

His sense of details and relentless rejection of biblical teaching astonished me, but once again I was cornered. I left because we were going broke and the lack of money was taking a toll on our marriage. Both of us were already considering other options outside of marriage and I feel that if we would have stayed, one, or both of us would have called it quits.

I would admit, I couldn't respond to Henry's question without telling him my whole life's story. God had been with us every step of the way and it wasn't that He didn't come through for us in Oklahoma City; it was that our faith needed a complete overhaul and our situation living between two sets of parents only prolonged, or even aggravated the situation. God had a plan for us, and knowing his great wisdom, I knew we needed to grow not just in faith, but as a couple.

"Sometimes you can be a real shithead Henry," I blurted out. Henry looked at me with a confused look on his face. That had been the first time he had heard me cuss since I picked him up at the truck stop in Kentucky.

For lack of a better response, he smiled with a hint of pride. "I'll take that as a compliment," he said. Just then the radio blared again in the small truck cab, the voice of Elvis in concert recorded live years earlier;

"Well I've never been to heaven, but I've been to Oklahoma. Well, they tell me I was born there, but I really don't remember."

Of course, neither Elvis or I were born in Oklahoma, but I can't help but wonder what went through Elvis' mind as he crossed this great state in his fully loaded, Cadillac station wagon with hundreds of miles of rolling grassy plains in all directions. It wasn't much to look at, but it had a beauty all its own. Here, you weren't boxed in by skyscrapers, trees or mountains. On the open prairies, you couldn't help but feel a sense of freedom in the very heart of big sky country. This was truly a slice of heaven.

"Next stop, Albuquerque, New Mexico," I announced as we again picked up our journey tracing the path of the historic Route 66 along the I-40. We had taken a long detour north and we were both glad to be back on the road again to Hollywood.

CHAPTER NINETEEN

Wise Men Say

O N MY MOTHER'S TWENTY-NINTH BIRTHDAY, April 19, 1972, an older; now mature Elvis stepped onto the stage at Tingley Coliseum in Albuquerque, New Mexico. He had not appeared there since 1956. Elvis had grown up. At 37 he had been in the army, gotten married and had a child.

There was no shortage of love for Elvis in this small U.S. city; the Tingley Coliseum was packed with nearly 12,000 screaming young women.

Elvis sang his last song of the night. The audience could not have known, it would be his final performance in Albuquerque.

"Wise men say, only fools rush in,

But I can't help, falling in love with you."

If God was with us on this long journey, he sure was keeping quiet; I knew where to find him. There was this little church in Albuquerque I had stopped at before several times. The church was run by a Pueblo Indian pastor called 'Church of the Nations Assembly of God'. The pastor was getting old and had chartered this Church as far back as the 1950s. The building resembled that of a stucco mission you might see in the middle of the desert, but this church was wedged between two huge strip malls a short distance away from the busy Interstate overpasses.

As luck would have it, it was Sunday and I usually tried to attend church somewhere every week regardless of the town I found myself in.

"You know you look like Elvis," said the dark skin Navajo pastor shaking my hand before entering the service. "You sing?" he asked.

"Yes, I do. I play the piano too," I said smiling as I tried not to stare at the deep cross-hatch of wrinkles on his forehead from years of preaching in this little church.

"Would you like to play for us this morning? We have a piano all setup and our pianist called in sick today."

I was shocked, to say the least at the added attention. Just behind him on a girded center post a short distance away, I caught a glimpse of myself in a gold framed mirror that hung from an old post nail. Even I was surprised at my appearance. I had changed, not just on the inside but on the outside, and for the first time, even I was beginning to see the resemblance to Elvis staring back at me. Maybe it was providence, maybe it was destiny; either way, I sensed my life was rounding a corner revealing the new, while the old dispensed quietly into the distance, in a place I thought I'd never be, in the most unlikely of circumstances.

"I would be honored Pastor—thank you."

His eyes were dark, deep-set and puffy with wrinkles that seemed to flow like microscopic canyons down over his rigid cheekbones. His forehead wrinkled up like ripples on a desert sand dune pelted with constant heat and wind that seemed charismatically accentuate every word he spoke. Everything about him seemed to resonate the wisdom of life that reflected his age and his humble sacrifice to the thousands of lives he had no doubt impacted over the years.

Henry Downer was sound asleep in the passenger seat of the big semi. I invited him in, also letting him know he was welcomed to stay in the truck. I was early enough to attend Sunday School, which gave me a lot of time to think about the troubled young man in the parking lot, several hundred yards away. His fierce atheism and lack of belief in God had struck a nerve with me and he had challenged everything I thought I believed in. At the same time, I had imagined him spending eternity in Hell, due at least in part, to my inability to share my faith in a practical way that would convince him to turn his life over to Christ.

"I must be a lousy Christian," I thought to myself, peering into the scratched bathroom mirror, checking my hair one more time before getting back onto the road. After hundreds of hours of driving over-the-road, I didn't look half bad. Perhaps it was the dry climate. I felt pretty good for a change, an improvement over the long, wet winters I was used to in Northern Washington. Something in me had clearly changed over the long haul from Florida. I had lots of time to think about my mistakes in life and realized, maybe things weren't as bad as I thought, at least compared to Henry who had no job, no real home. His kids abandoned him years earlier and left along with his ex-wife, he hadn't seen in over two years. It didn't appear that atheism was working very well for him.

The church sanctuary was very small and very quaint. As I walked toward the stage to take a seat at the piano, I could see a young Native American family sitting a few rows back. The kids were both smiling, and they were perfectly groomed. Something about this church just felt right, almost like I imagined I would feel stepping into heaven.

Pastor Jeremiah Nez started the service with a few announcements and then said, "We have a special guest this morning, 'Elvis is here with us all the way from Tennessee. He looked back and smiled. From behind the little electric piano, I raised my hand and waived, embarrassed to say the least."

He looked back at me and asked, "Jeffrey Elvis—do you know a song called *Crying in the Chapel*? Elvis used to sing that one." And there it was, just like that—*Jeffrey Elvis*; the name had a ring to it. I would just need to rearrange my real middle name a bit, but that would work. From that day forward, I would become Jeffrey Elvis. With that, I started to sing the old gospel tune along with the audience. Elvis would have been proud—I know I was proud of myself and somehow all the problems of life and mistakes I had made, began to drift away, like a ship fading over the horizon on a faraway destination.

> *"You saw me crying in the chapel, the tears I shed were tears of joy.*
>
> *I know the meaning of contentment, now I am happy with the Lord…*
>
> *Just a plain and simple chapel, where humble people go to pray.*
>
> *I pray the Lord that I'll grow stronger, as I live from day-to-day."*

It was about that time, the back double-doors of the church opened quietly as the bright light from the early morning sun over Albuquerque shined through the door causing several people in the audience to turn around and see what the distraction was, including the two little Navajo kids sitting near the front row. It was Henry. He looked bad, like he had just had a bad dream and had not slept in days. He winked at me then slid into a chair in the back row. The other band members looked over at me, curious over the connection between us.

"I know many of you young people, don't care much for some of those old songs, but I'm an old man and I really like those old hymns; old and dusty just like my black worn out suit coat.

Wasn't that nice?" Pastor Jeremiah said looking over at a now more skeptical audience of young parents and new believers. The youthful lead guitar player looked at the drum player and shrugged his shoulders hesitating to commit, but the rest of the audience nodded their heads in polite agreement.

Personally, I love that old song. It reminded me of my grandmother that used to sing next to me when I was a young child sitting on those old creaky wooden church benches, my feet barely touching the cold tile floor of the Navajo missionary church. Back then most of my family sang in the choir. When they would sing, you could hear all the harmony parts in unison echoing off the high vaulted cedar ceilings with sound flowing outward in all directions. Every Sunday, the choir loft was full, folks of all ages smiling just like the angels in heaven. That is where I learned to sing, at least the harmony parts. As some of you can tell, I wasn't the best singer in my day.

With a swipe of his forehead from a silky white handkerchief, Jeremiah started his ubiquitous sermon. It went something like this:

"Friends, I am Navajo, originally from the Navajo Indian reservation here in New Mexico. But I was no normal Navajo. No, I was not!" he said with acute distinction. I was a persecuted

Christian Navajo. My mother and I were beaten many times for our beliefs, but we didn't give up hope and we never stopped believing in the true almighty God. We didn't stray. We refused to worship the gods of the Navajo Indians." He spoke incredibly with an uncompromising conviction for a man that had been humbled by life and aged with the harshness of the desert New Mexico climate.

"I am eighty-five years old today," he said, as some of the audience clapped in response, "—and I refuse to stop preachin' the word of God. No, today is not the day because I'm still alive, and as long as there is blood in my veins, I will speak the words he tells me to speak!"

"You young ones are getting fed dope at school, leading you away from the truth. Your families keep changing churches to find one that best suits their needs, never considering what God's needs are. You know what? He doesn't need you to carry on his work, but he can use you. Don't you think you'd rather be working on a kingdom job for the King of Kings rather than sitting on a bench warming job listening as your hind side gets splinters from those old wooden benches you are finding so cozy—while thinking about those nice padded cushions to rest your lazy butt? Do you know what I'm talking about people?"

"I'm saying, you should be up here on this stage with me preachin'—I mean look at me, I could have a heart attack right here on this stage, and if I do—who will speak for me? Who is gonna tell the others about the love of Jesus? Who is gonna sing those dusty old hymns instead of those new, fancy, meaningless, self-seekin' songs churches are drawn into today? Who needs Jesus when you can heal yourself with a few simple 'feel good' songs that make your bones tingle and your ears ring, turned up loud to drown out your thinkin' with twenty-thousand watts of stereophonic amplification sound, all followed by a prerecorded video sermon by some national video production company from Reno Nevada? Who needs truth when you can make up your own religion? Who needs *Creation* when you can do everything for yourself?"

He paused for a moment to let the thought sink into the very depths of the souls of the now spellbound church members; some looking as if they had seen a ghost.

"Church, I'm here to tell you there is a creature that wanders the wilderness in the shadows of our own ignorance. He's black as coal with glowing red eyes and he sits in the shadows all night and all day, just waiting for you to take your eyes off Jesus. Well, he won't have to wait for very long will he? Especially for some you, I know, and you know I know!" At that moment, I thought about the black Alpaca I had seen in my dream as Jeremiah continued his rambling sermon.

"He will use guilt! He will use your finances! He will use your children—your job—your new home—and even your over inflated career aspirations, TO BRING YOU DOWN!" he yelled at the top of his lungs. The two little Navajo kids in the front row were now sitting straight up in their seats, listening attentively, afraid to even blink as Jeremiah continued his passionate, soul-gripping demonstration.

"Friends, all roads don't lead to God! The God of the Navajo Indians is not the god we worship today; no way. The tribal members that beat my mother nearly to death don't know Jesus. Jesus doesn't come to bring terror and fear into our households. He came to bring peace and I know there is one of you here today that needs peace in his or her life."

I don't know if it was a coincidence or not, but Jeremiah turned and looked me straight in the eye. His eyes seemed to glow like glistening gems, looking right through me like a tarnished crystal stained glass window, pierced by the vibrant rays of the morning sun.

"Guilty! You are Guilty!" he yelled. "How are you gonna let go of all that guilt?"

He paused for a moment as he could see a tear beginning to form around my eyelids. The audience was silent; you could hear a pin drop. No 'Hallelujahs'; no 'Praise Gods'; just silence as the gravity of the moment was laid squarely on my shoulders, like the broken bricks of an old mid-century warehouse.

"How could he know?" I asked myself. "That's simply not possible. He couldn't possibly be speaking straight to me." The thought-provoking implications of what was happening at that moment, sent a wave of goosebumps up my spine, rippling like shockwaves down my inner arm.

"You've got to let it go Jeffrey!" he said as he turned away, to my relief and started pointing with his thick trembling finger at the others in the eager audience. "You've got to let it go, Steve—you've got to let it go, Janice, —you've got to let it go and let Jesus… let Jesus heal you today!"

* * *

In 1974, Elvis walked on stage with an all new gold and white jumpsuit. It was unlike any he had worn before. On his chest was stitched an elaborate image of the ancient Mayan Calendar, an elaborate display of gold and bronze that took on a metallic sheen in the bright lights of the neon stage. There is no doubt that Elvis had strayed away from the teachings of his childhood; traditional teachings, replaced with more worldly variations of spirituality that involved ancient wisdom and mysticism.

Elvis and I truly share a common bond in seeking the truth and discovering the secrets of the universe. The Mayan Calendar was particularly interesting to me because it predicted the world would end December 22, of 2012. Of course, the world didn't end leaving spiritualist empty handed and grasping at straws, trying to find a new hook for their seemingly defrauded believers.

I felt the pastor had made a good point. He was right. All roads don't lead to God which explains how I made it to Albuquerque on-time for church on Sunday. I stuck to I-40 all the way and didn't take any out-of-the-way detours.

The service wrapped up with pastor Jeremiah saying a lengthy prayer. Then I sang a few more songs with the band before the final announcements inviting members to stay for coffee and cookies, available after the service in the back hallway.

Jeremiah continued. "If you need prayer or if you are ready to give it up for Jesus and start your life anew on the road that leads to truth, come now… don't put it off. I might be dead tomorrow and you might not get another chance! Next Sunday, Lord willing, I'm gonna be right up here preachin'. There's no shutting me up, no sir. See you next week," he said setting his mic carefully back in the stand.

I stopped playing after a few minutes and I noticed Henry walking down the aisle towards the pastor. I walked forward to greet him. I felt a nagging voice that seemed to be speaking to me from deep within; a quiet prompting beneath the layers of scars that covered hidden secrets, long since given way to guilty feelings of regret, unacknowledged even by my own conscious memories.

"Ask him now", the voice beckoned. "Right Now!"

"Are you ready to turn your life over to Jesus," I said boldly to Henry.

"Yes, I am," he said.

"That's it, you don't want to think about it?" I said, still stunned by his sudden presumptuous response.

"I'm ready—let's do it!"

The pastor stepped over and together we placed hands on

Henry's shoulders. He wasn't the only one saved that day. The remaining baggage of my own life that I had held onto for so many years, seemed to just fall off like shadows over a shallow morning lake bed at first light. I was finally free. I would leave everything at the altar that day, never to look back again. I realized, there was no substitute for God's healing power and grace. There is no philosophy or belief system you can adopt that replaces the power of true forgiveness that only Jesus himself offers—everything else is counterfeit:

> *For "I have seen all the works that are done under the sun; and behold, all is vanity and a chasing after wind," Ecclesiastes 1:14.*

CHAPTER TWENTY

Goodbye to Hollywood

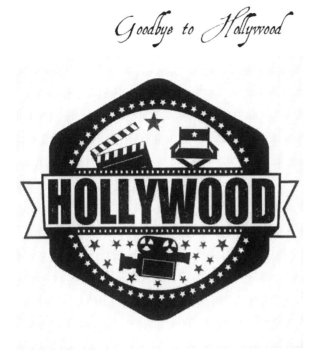

O KAY HOLLYWOOD, next stop is yours," I said loudly as we drove down the wide stretch of crowded freeway that would take us through the very heart of the busy, seemingly infinite hundred-mile long stretch of the Los Angeles valley basin. This was the end of the journey portrayed in John Steinbeck's 1962 novel, 'Grapes of Wrath,' bringing to an end, the torturous Route 66 highway that stretched out across the nation, all the way from Oklahoma City to somewhere in this vicinity, a marvelous plateau, now hidden by miles of strip malls and mega-freeways.

The overwhelming feeling of entering such a massive infrastructure is equally intimidating as it was during the Great Depression of the late 1920's. Although the city looked much different back then, there were still too many people competing for too few dwindling resources. I have often wondered if the immigrants from Oklahoma, Kansas, and Nebraska stayed here, or did they leave at the end of the ten-year Midwest famine and return to their dust filled homes? Considering the immense sea of people that stretched from Santa Clarita all the way to Santa Ana, I'm guessing at least some of those families are still here somewhere. Perhaps Henry was a distant relative of one of the families that settled here after crossing the most dismal terrain in the United States.

Henry woke up clearing his head and started gathering his things. The closest I could get to Hollywood was an overpass leading to his neighborhood where he supposedly had some friends to stay with. As best as I could make of it, his family members didn't want him around because he was difficult, and they blamed him for his divorce.

"So—Henry," I asked. "In a few minutes, I will drop you off and probably never see you again. We had ridden together for over two-thousand miles arguing everything from Christianity to Global

Warming. You haven't taken in a single word I've said the entire trip. What prompted your decision to turn your life over to Christ in that middle of nowhere, Native American church in Albuquerque, New Mexico?"

"You converted me?" he said. "Everyone is always trying to convert me. My ex-wife tried to convert me—but you actually did it," he said.

"You know Henry; you were an atheist less than twenty-four hours ago. I would have had better luck winning a million dollars in a slot machine in Vegas than converting you to anything, let alone Christianity. If anyone has built a case for atheism, you have done it, my friend."

I was starting to wonder who had converted who. He had cornered me on every single argument and made me feel ignorant and foolish in my knowledge of the world at every turn.

"I never got a word in edgewise with you and yet, you turned your back on your pride and made the decision to follow Christ," I said in amazement. I wasn't sure I was relieved or disappointed.

The next big green highway sign ahead said 'Hollywood', which meant it would only a be few minutes before reaching the overpass where he would need to be dropped off. He pulled out a long slim cigarette from his little red pack and wedged it between his teeth as if he were planning to light it. He paused a moment in thoughtful reluctance, then crushed the cigarette in his hand and tossed it out the window. The broken cigarette disappeared instantly from sight under the large, long-haul tires of the eighteen-wheeler.

"To tell you the truth, there is something about you that is different. I detected it almost immediately in that little theater during the Elvis movie at the Pilot Flying J. I could never quite put my finger on it until now. I sat out in the rain for two days trying to get a ride from anyone. I would never admit it, but I was desperate, hungry, and broke with no place to go. When I saw your truck pulling out of the parking lot, I knew you would stop. I can't explain it—I just knew." He continued, "Had you never said a single word to me the entire trip, I was already a believer, and I wanted what you had."

The Bible has very little to say about Darwinism, Evolution, American politics or half-a-dozen other topics we discussed along the road, but I was reminded of a verse that I memorized in Sunday School when I was a child, that says:

"If anyone asks that you carry his gear for a mile, carry it two miles. Give to those who ask, and don't turn away from those who want to borrow," Matthew 5:41-42.

"You would do well to stick to what you believe and don't worry about all the worldly stuff. It's like you said…it's hopeless. Become the person God made you to be, and you'll do alright. Who knows, maybe someday you'll write a book about it," he said with a wink as he worked his way out the door and onto the pavement of the long overpass that extended over the ten-lane freeway. I could just make out his words over the loud thunder of the vehicles below.

He came around and shook my hand through the window then hurried off into the busy district. I glanced up to check the traffic light to see if it had turned green, then looked back to take one last look at Henry. He had simply vanished into the background of the enormous concrete and steel metropolis known as, the 'City of Angels'.

I glanced over at the passenger seat and noticed he had left his prescription glasses behind. I yelled out the window, but it was too late. The light had turned green and I had to get back on the crowded freeway. His glasses are all that remained of my memory of Henry. I kept them with me for nearly a year and they helped me to see more clearly; which in some way is ironic. I thought of him each time I put them on, wondering how he had made out; curious if I would ever run into him again, if not on the streets of gold that lined the outer reaches of heaven's eternal highway.

CHAPTER TWENTY-ONE

What Happens in Vegas

THAT AFTERNOON, I picked up what would be my final load back to Salt Lake City Utah. I stopped in Las Vegas where I stayed the night. The lights and the activity of Vegas are mesmerizing, and I can see why Elvis liked it here. I walked all over that amazing City of Lights until nearly 4 a.m. studying the grand architecture in the warm evening desert air. Little did I know that I would be back here two years later to perform at *Sam's Club* with twenty-five Elvis Tribute contestants competing for $5000 in prize money.

Elvis' later years are left to us for speculation and interpretation surrounding his untimely demise. However, hundreds of eyewitness testimonies have surfaced over the years that tell their side of the story following his death in 1978.

I believe Elvis may have lost his way in this world, that I am sure of. His amazing talent and humble generosity stretched across the nation and around the world, even beyond the barren desert landscape of Las Vegas, a city that now lights the desert like the stars of a distant galaxy. Today his presence can still be felt there, and so it will be; as long as there is light in the heavens and music in the darkest of nights.

Elvis' fame circled the globe. Much of his wealth, he gave away, including more than $26 million to build the memorial for the war veterans of Pearl Harbor in Hawaii, an underwater rusting battleship that can be viewed by tourists, even to this day. Despite his success, Elvis lived a lonely and isolated existence towards the end, unable to leave his hotel room without getting mobbed by crazed fans and overzealous paparazzi photographers, eager to capture a glimpse of the King of Rock & Roll.

I am left to ponder, who would give Elvis a ride when he was stranded along the road in the rain, in the middle of nowhere? Who'd carry him, when there was no one else to help him along the way? Who would step aside from their self-centered existence for just a moment, to make sure he had a passenger window and a pillow with which to lay his head. Maybe that person will be you!

* * *

"In the last days, there will be very difficult times. For people will love only themselves and their money. They will be boastful and proud, scoffing at God, disobedient to their parents, and ungrateful.

...and they will act religious, but they will reject the power that could make them godly." —2 Timothy 3:1-5.

THE GOD BOX

ENCORE

Graves

The following chapter was not included in the original storyline, but I kept it in for your enjoyment or displeasure, whichever the case may be. "Thank you very" much for reading—Enjoy

O N A SMALL QUIET GRASSY PLOT OF LAND, next to a growing mound of soft, freshly excavated dirt, two gravediggers were finishing up their work for the day at the Forest Hill Cemetery, just east of Memphis, Tennessee. It was here, more than forty years earlier that Elvis Presley was laid to rest in a mausoleum, just a short distance away. More than 75,000 people from all over the nation migrated here during the days following his untimely death to pay their respects.

"Well Joe, I guess we'll be working some overtime tonight," said Gordan, finishing up the last of his unfiltered, hand-rolled cigarette, held snuggly between two bony fingers that dangled from his aged-spotted hands. He was taking a quick break while he watched the other man dig out the last few shovels of dirt from the six-foot box-shaped graveyard ditch. They had spent most of that afternoon digging by hand since their tractor was broken down, and they would not have time to get it fixed before the scheduled funeral ceremonies commenced that afternoon.

I was standing at the bottom of the six-foot ditch, giving the gravediggers a hand, helping them in and out of the deepening hole. There was something about being this far underground that I hated. Looking up, I could see just the edges of the remaining grass at the mouth of the large opening that loomed over me like a dense fog, closing in around me. The smell of dirt reminded me of an old house I once played in when I was child. Small roots and stones, lined the perfectly dug sides of the trench, and although it was a sweltering day outside, it stayed a cool sixty-five degrees just below the surface.

Looking down, I could feel my bright white polished formal shoes, squishing against the soft dirt and sand at the bottom of a large opening, soon to become the permanent resting place for some unlucky cadaver. In one corner, I could see a small black beetle attempting to climb the wall, but to no avail. I shook off a small spider that had worked its way onto my right shoe.

"I hate spiders," I thought to myself.

"Guys, I'm getting really dirty down here, can you help me out of this hole?" I said, looking up at the now curious wrinkled face of Gordan, showing signs of some concern. My white jumpsuit had just been cleaned the day before, now it was dirty again, grass stains on the knees and spots all up and down the sides of my legs and thighs. The large white and gold belt buckle that had inspired many audiences in nearly half a decade of shows no longer sparkled this far down below the earth's surface. The afternoon sun was already casting a gloomy shadow on the sides of the nearly completed pit.

"What's your name, sir?" I asked the dark cold faced gravedigger who was now standing up, finishing his last cigarette. He flicked the lit butt down into the hole which landed on my shoulder, spewing ashes down the top of my gold studded jumpsuit. The red, white, and blue gems were sewn into the fabric to form the shape of an American eagle. It was my favorite outfit and to say the least, I wasn't happy watching it get ruined at the hands of some lanky cemetery workers.

"Hey mister," I yelled, from the bottom of the ditch, "—knock that off. Get me out of here before it gets dark," I insisted. Now both Gordan and Joe were looking down at me at the bottom of the ditch. They both looked confused.

"You can't come out, you're dead," said Joe.

"Yea, you're dead," said Gordan agreeing with his friend.

"Seriously, do I look dead to you?" I said standing there plain as day.

"You wanted to know what it was like to be Elvis didn't you," said Joe. "Now's your chance to find out".

"Well yes of course," I said, "but don't you think we are taking this a little too far?"

Joe stood up and grabbed a shovel full of dirt and threw it on me. The dusty dirt covered my eyes, blinding me momentarily, coating the top of my head with a plume of gritty sand and bits of fine, sun-bleached clay. I shook what dirt I could out of my hair, then looked up at the stranger and angrily shook my fist at him. He just looked at me and laughed.

"You guys are in big trouble," I yelled. "I want to speak to your boss right now!"

They looked at each other and chuckled. Now they were both shoveling dirt into the hole around me with even greater enthusiasm.

"Hey now...this isn't funny anymore! This is not what I bargained for," I said. "I am a singer—a professional," I continued, finding it increasingly difficult to keep my feet from getting stuck. I could hardly see through the dust and dirt being dumped on my head until I was nearly dormant, making it difficult to move with the mounting dirt, piling up all around me, covering the gold chains of my Elvis Aloha Hawaii belt buckle.

As I began to feel the dirt pressing against my chest making breathing difficult, I could faintly hear an Elvis song playing over the little black transistor radio just outside the mouth of the open grave.

"Maybe I didn't treat you, quite as good as I should have.

Maybe I didn't love you, quite as often as I could have.

Little things I should have said and done, I just never took the time.

You were always on my mind, you were always on my mind."

With a gasping breath, I yelled at the top of my lungs, "You can't do this. Get me the caretaker!"

* * *

I awoke suddenly in the afternoon; startled by the grinding transmission of another eighteen-wheeler that had parked next to me at a quiet rest stop along I-84, just south of the Utah-Idaho border. I had stopped to take a break from the long drive across southern Idaho. I was exhausted, although I wasn't in a hurry to get back to Salt Lake, knowing this would be my final journey with this truck before ending my career as a truck driver.

It was a hot breezy day. At the rest stop, you could look over the dry deserted valley of an old lake bed that would have extended as far away as Salt Lake City. Now it was a dry, dusty salt saturated flat that wasn't good for much of anything, other than cattle grazing.

On the far side of the desert plain, I could see a billowing gray storm cloud that was kicking dust up off the desert floor, whisking the tiny particles, high into the atmosphere where they collected moisture from the cool air, passing over the peaceful valley. Snowville Utah was my favorite stop on the way back to the Salt Lake central terminal. With a final glance at the fascinating storm in the distance, I hopped back into the truck cab once again, turned over the powerful diesel engine, and headed south.

As I approached the storm, I noticed other cars pulling to the side of the road and drivers getting out of their cars cleaning their windshields. Then mud began to rain from the sky as if God himself was pouring a bottle of brown chocolate syrup all over the front of my shiny red truck, leaving the windows coated and dripping with wet mud. Even the side mirrors instantly disappeared in an avalanche of rain-soaked dirt. I couldn't see anything, and my windshield wipers were defenseless against the pounding, sludgy film.

I pulled to the side of the road, hoping I would not be hit by another oncoming driver headed in the same direction, struggling to see through this bizarre weather phenomena. With a clean white T-shirt, I managed to clear at least some of the sludge off my windows and mirrors, but the truck looked like it had been driven through a muddy gravel pit.

Instead of heading all the way back to Salt Lake that day, I decided to spend one more night on the truck before calling it quits. In Snowville Idaho, I found a quiet place to park, next to one of my favorite cafes in the whole country, where I again fell sound asleep as soon as my head hit the pillow.

* * *

"You wanted the caretaker, well here I am," bellowed the voice of a stranger looking down at me in the six-foot grave that was rapidly becoming my permanent home. "What seems to be the problem?"

The gravediggers had stopped shoveling dirt into the ditch momentarily, and through the dust, I could scarcely make out the face of a tall slender, white-haired man with a narrow jaw. He looked something like Dick Van Dyke, only his cheekbones stood out a little further and his eyes were deeply set into his aging wrinkled forehead.

"Are you kidding or what? —just look at me! I'm covered in dirt, you moron. Of course, I have a problem…your gravediggers are trying to bury me alive!" I yelled, struggling to force more air into my pressing lungs, weighted by the heavy soil mounded against them.

The caretaker looked over at Joe and Gordan who looked puzzled as well. "Is he alive?" asked the caretaker looking a Joe, then at Gordan?

"No said Gordan," shaking his head, disgusted with having to respond to such a ridiculous question.

"Gordan says you're dead," said the caretaker.

"Look at me you idiot, can you hear my voice—can you see my lips moving—I'm not dead!" I said, coughing and choking as a small handful of dirt, fell at the edge of the grave, kicking up more dust as it fell into the wide basin.

Joe shrugged his shoulders, not sure what to think.

The caretaker bent over the mouth of the hole to get a better look. All he could see now was the top of my shoulders and the gold, red and white studs of the embroidered beads of my jumpsuit.

"What makes you think you're alive?" he asked.

"That is such a stupid question," I mocked, mustering up more fury as to what I was going to do to these guys when I got out of that big hole in the ground.

"Okay, bury him," said the caretaker as the gravediggers grabbed their shovels once again, ready to finish filling the hole back in with me in it.

"WAIT! WAIT!" I pleaded, "—please stop!".

The caretaker motioned his hand for the gravediggers to pause for a moment to hear what I had to say.

"I haven't got it right yet," I said humbly.

"What's that, you're mumbling," said the caretaker.

"I tell you he's dead," snarled Joe again, becoming increasingly annoyed.

"I haven't done the things I need to do yet," I said, tipping my head downward; feeling a tear begin to form in the dust and dirt that encircled my eyelid.

"So, what is so important that I have to pay my gravediggers overtime wages to dig you out of there? Can't you see they are tired and ready to go home? It's been a long day," he said, as Joe and Gordan nodded their heads in agreement.

"I have to make things right. I need another chance," I said, watching that little spider I had kicked off my shoe, wander onto my left shoulder. I tried to shrug him off, but it was hopeless. I was wedged in too tightly to move.

"Make things right, how?" inquired the caretaker. "Your wife says your selfish, your kids don't know you anymore, and your mother; who is paying these gravediggers to dig this hole, didn't feel she wanted to spring for a casket. She must have thought that was included in the burial price...not so—as you can clearly see," he said accusingly.

"You have wasted your life and now here you are, a thousand miles from home waiting for life to happen...well let me tell you something sir, you have missed your chance."

"I wrote a book—doesn't that count for something?" I pleaded.

"I've read your silly book—here it is," he replied, tossing a badly worn paperback into the ditch. I recognized the book as a copy of one I had written less than a year earlier. It was the story of my life.

"You should read your own books some time...now you'll have all the time in the world." The book wasn't exactly a best seller. "Who knows, you might learn something down there," he said, with a smirk that preceded an evil grin.

"Yes, I know—I get that. I understand everything now. I know what I need to do to get it right. Every minute of my life is precious, and I know I need to cherish every single breath. Everything...every day—every minute." I continued my desperate plea with the caretaker with a life-sentence in eternity, hanging in the balance.

"Now please, just dig me out so I can prove to everyone that I'm not the jerk they thought I was. I can make a difference—I can make it better—I can—I know that now!" I added.

Joe looked up at the skeptical caretaker once again and shrugged his shoulders. Gordan glanced over at Joe, and then at the caretaker.

"Seen enough?" asked Joe, watching the caretaker's expression which seemed somehow less confused than it had been just minutes ago.

"Yeah—I've seen enough," said the caretaker turning to walk away.

"Well that's that," commented Gordan grabbing his shovel. "Looks like you're too late," he said, with a final murky wink at Joe.

"WAIT, HOLD ON!" I yelled once more as the sound of shovels, dug into the remaining dirt pile that lined the sides of the grave. "—I'm the main character—I'm not supposed to die."

"Elvis Presley died, and he was bigger'n you!" said Joe tossing a healthy scoop towards the side of the ditch to fill in the corner just a few feet from my head.

"Elvis didn't die—they faked his death," I said, squinting to keep my eyes open.

I could hear the two men laughing to themselves. "We buried him too," he said. "At least he left us a few good records. All you got is this book—good luck with that."

The book the caretaker had thrown into the ditch, landed right next to my face. The binder had sprung open and I could just make out the text on what I recognized was the very last page of my fabled book. It read:

"THE END."

"Elvis has left the building."

EPILOGUE

I N A PRIVATE DRESSING ROOM, of a small town gymnasium, I was making a few last minute adjustments to my hair and my newly acquired 68' leather outfit, a replica from the 'Elvis' Comeback' tour shipped from Mumbai, India. I could hear the low rumble of the crowd spread across the gym floor and the squeaky creaks of the nearly packed hardwood and steel framed bleachers. I had memorized every detail of the performance that would commemorate the memory and life of Jake Maberry, one of the best-known coaches in the history of sports in this little Dutch town of Lynden Washington.

"It's time," called a voice from just outside the door. I took a deep breath and said a quick prayer as I ran my fingers over the little gold cross that hung around my neck. It had been nearly two years since I had turned in my big red box semi-truck to the central terminal in Salt Lake City, Utah.

I had always believed God would restore the wealth we had lost during the recession but after leaving the trucking company we were still struggling. As I set foot on the stage I looked at the thousands of people who had shown up for the memorial service. I knew at this moment that God had given back more than I had lost during the Great Recession. Our recovery however, did not come in the manner I had expected; neither money nor possessions. God had given me back my family and had blessed me with an incredible voice to share with the thousands of people over the years that followed.

With my 1950's Elvis mic in hand, I said a brief word to the audience to introduce the single solo gospel song I was to sing.

"I'm sure Jake would be proud of this high school's legendary sports program many of you have helped to achieve—but knowing Jake, he also would have said that some of you are still sitting on the bench, even after all these years. You're not using the good gifts God has given you. You're not using your head," as he would say.

From what I know about Jake, he was an A-team guy and I'm sure he would want all of you to join him someday—and I mean join that great big A-Team in the sky." I paused for a moment to let my words sink in while the intro of, 'How Great Thou Art' began to play in the background.

I continued, "While I sing this next song, I want you to take a moment to think about where your life is headed. You still have a brief time to take the exit off that superhighway that is taking you down the wrong road, in the wrong direction that leads nowhere. To be on the A-Team, you gotta take the narrow road. Please stand and join me as I sing this legendary gospel song—I'm sure most of you know the words."

> *"Oh Lord my God, when I in awesome wonder, consider all the worlds thy hands have made. I see the stars, I hear the rolling thunder. Thy power throughout, the universe displayed. Then sings my soul, my Savior, God, to Thee. How great thou art. How great thou art."*

— In memory of Jake Maberry (1930 – 2017).

Several weeks later, my daughter and my son graduated from high school. They graduated from the same school I had graduated from thirty-five years earlier. A rainbow hovered over the school for nearly two hours while the ceremony took place in the same gymnasium I had sung just two weeks earlier. I was reminded that the rainbow was a symbol of God's promise to never again flood the earth. For me, it symbolized the promise I had made during my truck driving years; to spend more time with my children and learn to sing

THE GOD BOX

Elvis—like nobody's business.

168

AFTERWARD

I N DECEMBER OF 2017, a guest pastor came to preach at the Whatcom New Life, Assemblies of God church in Ferndale Washington; a church I had been attending since I quit truck driving several years earlier. The special speaker's name was Jamie Montoya who had been an evangelical preacher for more than seventeen years after a radical conversion from a life of drugs and addiction. At first, he was not familiar to me but as he began to speak, I recognized his preaching style.

"Can you do something bold today," he said. "Can everyone stand up and just reach your hands to heaven. Many people in our country have heard of God but don't see Him as a way of solving their problems and becoming Lord in their lives. Today I want you to open that door and let him know that you want to begin doing things His way. Pray for the openness to hear his word and allow Him to begin helping you use the unique gifts God has given you."

He tipped his head and began to pray, "Jesus, today is my day. Speak to me and transform me by your word. Give me eyes to see, ears to hear and a heart and a mind that's ready, willing and able to believe and receive every word that you would speak into my existence. I give you full permission and access to do only what you can do in me. From this moment on, you have my full undivided attention. Have your way in me Lord—Amen."

As I sat there in my chair several rows back from the front, I realized I had heard this sermon before. It had been nearly five years since I last drove long-haul across the country but at that moment, I distinctly recalled the style of the preaching and the impact the sermon was having on the audience. His head was now completely shaved smooth and his eyes were set deep and dark into their sockets. His conviction was impenetrable, and his words were undeniably prophetic.

You see, in Florence Alabama the day after I had gone fishing on the dock just below the small river city, I attended a small Assemblies of God Church on Sunday as I often did during those years. They had a guest pastor speaking that day that had a profound effect on me. Before the sermon was over, most of the congregation was on their knees in front of this little church. Some weeping, some praying and some raising their hands to heaven in praise.

I was baffled by the whole thing but would not leave my seat, too ashamed of my life to go forward. I felt God had rejected me and was punishing me for my mistakes which I felt at the time I most certainly deserved. The pastor looked over the now empty rows in front of me with those deep-set eyes and I could see nothing but compassion in them; compassion for me. It could not have been more than a few seconds, but his subtle glance in my direction, spoke volumes.

After the service in that small humble Florence church, I finally went forward and told him my story of how I had screwed everything up and lost twenty years of family wealth making some very bad decisions. Greed and selfishness had taken me to the end of my rope and now here I was nearly 3000 miles from home, wanting my life back and another chance to make things right. It was then that he reached his hand out and placed it firmly on my shoulder and it was then that I asked God to give me another chance.

As Jamie began speaking in the Ferndale church in December approaching the holidays in 2017, five years and three thousand miles from our first encounter, I realized that I was witnessing a miracle; an impossible sequence of events that had taken me to the end of my journey that had lasted more than seven years; a moment that I could not let my book go to print without recognizing. This was the same pastor who had prayed for me clear across the county at my lowest moment, a day that set me on a path of healing that was only in its infancy.

In disbelief, I asked him if he had ever spoken in Florence, Alabama at a small *Assemblies of God* church there. He said he had on occasion as a substitute for their regular pastor who was on vacation that Sunday. Strange as it may sound, he remembered me even though my appearance had changed considerably over the years that followed.

I knew at that moment, I had gotten the message God was trying to get through to me all along. I had kept my promise to raise my kids and sing wherever I could with a voice I can only explain as

God-given. I also realized that this was the end of this amazing journey.

We shook hands and he caught a plane later that day. I knew it would be unlikely I would ever see him again. He had taken up, just a moment of time in my life, and yet he had made all the difference. I quietly hoped I could have the same impact on others someday.

"You are not here by accident, you are here by divine appointment. God has a whole lot of things he is wanting to do in your life, things he has planned from the very beginning."—Jamie Montoya

WHO WOULD HAVE THOUGHT?

ACKNOWLEDGEMENTS

I would like to thank my *fans, editors, managers, mentors and customers* that provided the powerful inspiration behind this incredible story. You have all, made it possible to keep the Jeffrey Elvis show alive and thriving in the upper most reaches of North America, the U.S. and Canada. I would particularly like to thank my close friend Mike French who provided much of the inciteful guidance along the way. Mike encouraged me to revisit the roots of my faith and focus on my religious beginnings, much like Elvis Presley would have done in his early gospel years. I don't consider myself to be an Elvis historian, but wherever possible I have tried to keep the Elvis historical facts straight, thanks to the many websites dedicated to his legendary life.

Thanks to my mother who has followed my career all along the way through thick and thin. I'm very thankful for the many hours she has spent editing and re-editing my stories for which we both feel a deep connection.

In addition, I would like to thank my earliest fans from the very beginning: Rita Buhr, Inez Petersen and Demetree Robinson, Ann Carlson, Lynde Dorscher: photographer, Connie Van Dyken Hoag, Jay Barry: tour manager, Whitney Mcelroy: Point Roberts *Compass*

Rose Bar and Grill, Randall Sheriff at *"The Beach" Restaurant:* Home of *Jeffrey Elvis* in Blaine, Andrea Lynne who inspired my original song, *"Road to Nowhere"*; the *Silver City Band* (*Bruce, Jeffrey, Greg and Victor*) and the *Central Refrigerated* trucking company in Salt Lake City who provided my employment, during the *Great Recession*.

Last but certainly not least, my wife Nancy who has put up with it all for more than 30 years...being married to Jeffrey Elvis is no picnic...but it has been fun.

Behind every successful man, there is a woman rolling her eyes.
—*Jim Carrey*

Thanks to everyone...thank you very much. This book is being marketed using social media and cannot be successful unless you tell a friend...or better yet, give them a book...it just might change their life forever!

MIKE FRENCH

INSPIRATIONAL PUBLISHER/SPEAKER

WWW.POWERPACKEDPROMISES.COM

BOOKING INFORMATION

WWW.JEFFREYELVIS.COM

Made in the USA
Columbia, SC
20 February 2018